SELF-LOVE WORKBOOK
FOR FIRST-TIME MOMS

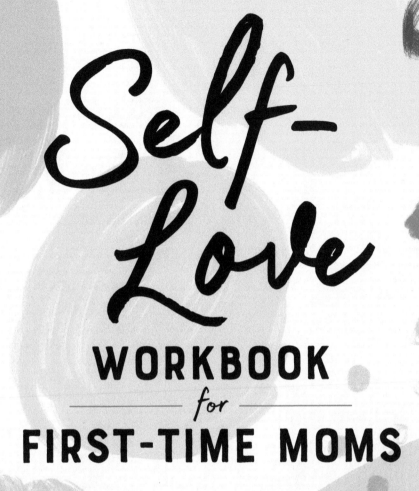

Self-Love

WORKBOOK

for

FIRST-TIME MOMS

A Road Map to Falling in Love with Yourself Again

ELSA ROJAS, PhD, PMH-C

ROCKRIDGE
PRESS

For general information on our other products and services or to obtain technical support, please contact our Customer Care Department within the United States at (866) 744-2665, or outside the United States at (510) 253-0500.

Rockridge Press publishes its books in a variety of electronic and print formats. Some content that appears in print may not be available in electronic books, and vice versa.

Interior and Cover Designer: Angie Chiu
Art Producer: Megan Baggott
Editor: Mo Mozuch
Production Editor: Mia Moran
Production Manager: Martin Worthington
Illustrations: The Noun Project, pp. 33, 34; Saifurrijal / The Noun Project, pp. 40, 142; Mu'as / The Noun Project, p. 139
Author photo courtesy of Sylvia Mier

ISBN: Print 978-1-64876-962-7
eBook 978-1-64876-963-4
R0

THIS WORKBOOK BELONGS TO

_____

You alone are enough.
You have nothing to prove
to anybody.

—MAYA ANGELOU

contents

introduction

Welcome to the wonderful world of parenthood!

No matter the reason, I am so glad you have picked up this book and decided to take a look around. My goal in writing this is to provide a useful tool to help first-time moms let go of self-doubt and judgment and learn to fully embrace themselves.

This book is not about only embracing positive emotions. I do not have a magic spell to erase any painful thoughts or unwanted images from your mind. I am not going to tell you how to lose weight, or even how to make sure you are a "good mom." This is not a book about "fixing" yourself or making changes to help you be worthy of self-love. This is a book about loving your whole self, as you are, no matter what.

When you first become a mom, so much changes! Your relationships with your partner, friends, and family have to grow to accommodate your new child. If you gave birth, your body and your hormones may still be changing. And no matter how you became a mom (birth, adoption, surrogacy, marriage), it is quite possible you are noticing changes in your ability to think clearly, keep your eyes dry, and feel accomplished in your day-to-day life. Given all this, it's easy to lose sight of how strong, resilient, and powerful you are. Yes, you! This is a book about helping you connect to a place of self-love and to see yourself with less judgment. It's about learning to accept that you will make mistakes, and knowing you remain powerful and wonderful on your best days, your worst days, and every day in between.

Why would I write a book about this? Well, because there is so much advice out there encouraging moms to always focus on the bright side: "Be glad your baby is healthy." "You're so lucky she is sleeping well." "At least your partner is supportive." The list goes on. These messages often teach moms that feeling unhappy and stressed isn't okay. Furthermore, there is so much advice about how to "get your body back" or how to magically fix your child's sleep troubles with this or that product. These messages make it easy for doubtful moms to judge themselves, which pulls them away from self-love. I wrote this book because I believe all mothers deserve to feel good about themselves. In my life, the more I am connected to an inner sense of self-love and acceptance, the more I can engage in ways that help me grow and connect with others. This, in turn, strengthens my sense of self-love. I want you to learn how to approach yourself from a place of love.

However, this book is not a replacement for therapy or seeking medical treatment. For some readers, this book may be all you need. Others may want to seek additional support, and I have included a list of resources at the end of the book to help. Remember, seeking therapy is a sign of immense strength. As a therapist, I know it is difficult to reach out for help, and if you need to, I really hope you will.

No matter what, I hope you take the time to move through this workbook at your own pace. In the pages ahead, you will find a number of elements, including prompts to help you reflect, exercises designed to teach new skills, practices you can try, and quotes and affirmations I hope inspire you. There is no rush, and no right way to approach the task of developing self-love. Some of the pages and exercises may speak to you, others may not, and still others might feel painful or challenging. I hope you will allow yourself to be vulnerable and find time to practice and reflect as you move through this work. Cultivating a sense of self-love takes time and effort. The goal of this workbook is to help you on your journey.

I was once afraid of people saying, "Who does she think she is?" Now I have the courage to stand and say, "This is who I am."

—OPRAH WINFREY

PART ONE

THE IMPORTANCE OF SELF-LOVE

To start, I want to take a moment to talk about the path ahead. While you don't have to go through this workbook in order, there is a purpose to the order of things. In part 1, my goal is to give you a clear understanding of what self-love is, what it isn't (hint: it's not just positive thinking), and why improving your self-love is so important as you adjust to life as a new (or not-so-new) parent. I'll also highlight some of the common barriers you're likely to face and offer motivation as you continue on this path.

To be a good parent, you need to take care of yourself so that you can have the physical and emotional energy to take care of your family.

—MICHELLE OBAMA

one.

LOVING YOUR CHILD, LOVING YOURSELF

Self-love seems both easy to understand and impossible to define and put into action. Sure, you know what the individual words mean, and I'm willing to bet you are pretty good at loving others. Loving yourself, though—that's often a bit more difficult. In fact, sometimes when we really try to love ourselves, it can feel uncomfortable or even painful. This is because learning to love ourselves forces us to recognize the lack of self-love we have been experiencing. I encourage you to allow yourself to notice this and to keep moving forward even when it feels painful, because it won't always be that way. As you move forward, I hope you'll really start to understand what it looks like to love yourself and why self-love is such an important asset to you as a first-time mom.

WHAT DOES SELF-LOVE MEAN?

In my experience as a psychologist (and as a human), I find people often have wildly different definitions of self-love. However, for this book, self-love can be defined as *the acceptance, compassion, respect, and admiration we show ourselves.*

Now, it's possible I just made this more complicated by adding a whole set of new words to define, but please, hang in there with me. When we love others, we *accept* them. We know our friends and loved ones aren't perfect, and we do our best to accept and love them even when we know they are making mistakes. We show our friends and family *compassion* when we treat them kindly, even on their worst days. For example, if your friend snaps at you after she's had a horrible day at work, you forgive her because you know she is stressed. We *respect* our loved ones when we listen to their opinions, even if we disagree, and we *admire* them by celebrating their accomplishments. Self-love is about showing up for yourself in these same ways—accepting all the unique parts of yourself, being gentle with yourself, believing you are worthy, and recognizing your achievements, big and small. You do it for others, and it's time to do it for you.

WHAT DOES SELF-LOVE MEAN FOR A FIRST-TIME MOM?

Motherhood is a beautiful thing. It is also a difficult, challenging, unknowable thing. It's not something that can be done perfectly, but it can feel like the stakes are so high that it's scary to allow yourself to be human. This is where self-love comes in. For first-time moms, self-love is an important tool to help you move toward feeling comfortable and more confident as you navigate this whole parenthood thing. Self-love is the reservoir you will draw from to remind yourself you are good enough, and it will be a key part of allowing yourself to grow into this new role. A mom who can love herself will be able to weather the ups and downs of learning to be a parent. A mom who loves herself will be able to take care of herself, knowing her well-being is critical to her success. For first-time moms, self-love means being gentle with yourself as you learn and strong enough to recognize how amazing you already are.

WHY IS IT SO HARD FOR US TO LOVE OURSELVES?

Self-love can be difficult for many reasons. For some, it can feel dangerous. They worry loving themselves will become an excuse for not growing and changing, or it will lead to "selfish behavior." For others, self-love can feel painful because they aren't sure it's something they deserve. People often think they need to accomplish some set of tasks or reach some goal before they deserve to feel good about themselves or treat themselves with kindness.

All of this can put self-love out of reach. You can go long periods without showing yourself care, respect, or compassion. Then, when you do finally open yourself up to self-love, it can feel painful because you are finally noticing and accepting emotions you have pushed out of the way for so long.

Do your best to accept any anxious feelings, and try to adopt a different attitude toward self-love. View it as something we are all worthy of, simply for being human. Allow yourself to recognize you are imperfect, you are learning, and you are deserving of both forgiveness and encouragement.

Why Self-Love Is a Challenge for Women and Moms

One major factor for many women is the social pressure to focus on others. This is not unique to mothers. Many women feel it is their job to care for others (siblings, parents, partners) and struggle to make themselves a priority. This only increases with motherhood. Many moms, especially first-time moms, feel the need to focus all their energy on their child. You may also notice pressure to live up to certain expectations or to parent a certain way. This makes taking time to focus on self-love difficult; however, it is still critical that you do.

BEING A FIRST-TIME MOM IS HARD

No matter how you became a mom, taking on the role for the first time is a pretty monumental task. If you are mothering an infant, you are dealing with the day-to-day tasks of keeping your tiny human alive and healthy. Even with a helpful partner and support system, many moms find themselves frequently worried and overwhelmed by the responsibility of caring for a new baby.

If you have become a first-time mom through adoption or as a stepmom, you may be starting this journey with older children. They may be able to go to the bathroom without you, but they still need just as much. The task of caring for, and teaching, young children and teens can be every bit as challenging and requires significant emotional energy. No matter where you are on your journey through motherhood, it is okay to find things difficult. Learning your new role takes time and patience, especially as a first-time mom.

A Massive Transformation and Life Transition

This stage of your life is a major (and difficult) transition. Anthropologist Dana Raphael actually coined a term for this—*matrescence*. The word refers to the process of becoming a mother and all the emotional, physical, and psychological changes involved. Like any other life transition (think adolescence/puberty), these changes can be both welcome and unwanted at the same time. Struggling doesn't make you a "bad mom" or mean anything is wrong. You are growing, and that requires some growing pains.

Loss of Personal Identity

Becoming a first-time mom can feel like losing yourself. You may find so much of your attention is focused on your baby that you forget other parts of yourself. Worse yet, others may stop asking you about yourself. This can be painful, but remember the role of "mom" is only one part of who you are. As you learn to love yourself more, you can give yourself permission to invest in the other areas of your identity that make you *you*.

Loss of Control over Your Time and Energy

Becoming a mother also means your day is no longer just yours; it belongs, in part, to your child. It means you'll need to find ways to let yourself off the hook when you can't get the dishes done, shower, or tend to other tasks in quite the same way you used to. It will be important to remember you are not lazy or failing if you don't respond to that email as quickly as you might have in your pre-baby life.

Societal Pressure of Being a "Good" Mom

Another aspect making this stage of life so difficult is social expectations. You were probably dealing with the pressure to be a "good" mom even before your child arrived. There seem to be lots of "rules," whether you are trying to conceive, learning to be a stepparent, or adopting. This pressure tends to breed self-doubt and push you toward self-critical thinking. The louder the voices telling you to "do more" and do it the "right way" are, the harder it can become to treat yourself with compassion, respect, and admiration.

Mental, Physical, and Emotional Exhaustion

No matter how you prepared for motherhood, it is not really possible to be ready for all the ways this new role will exhaust you, physically, emotionally, and mentally. It makes it difficult for you to feel like yourself, and you'll question your capability and sanity (especially when foggy-headed "mommy brain" kicks in). It can contribute to feelings that you are lazy or not strong enough, especially when the end of the day comes and you still haven't finished your to-do list.

Postpartum Mood
and Anxiety Disorders

Most people have heard of postpartum depression, but many difficulties can arise during and after pregnancy. Mental health professionals call them perinatal mood and anxiety disorders, or PMADs. So, if you are crying frequently, experiencing mood swings, or having trouble sleeping, especially past the first two to three weeks postpartum, it would be a good idea to talk to a medical provider you trust.

It's also important to note that while birth can be empowering and positive, many new moms will describe their birth experience as traumatic, according to research published in *Clinical Obstetrics and Gynecology* in 2004. There are many reasons for this, including lack of support from the medical team, a feeling of not being listened to, complications during birth, and past trauma. Notably, most people who describe their birth experience as traumatic will leave the hospital healthy and with a healthy baby. The good news? Trauma and PMADs are very treatable.

Here are a few signs you may need more support:

* If you had a difficult or traumatic experience. This could mean anything from a pregnancy loss to mistreatment by medical staff or a medical emergency during birth.

* If you find it difficult to reflect on the story of your child's birth, experience strong feelings of distress when you are reminded of the birth, or notice changes to how you think about yourself or the world (e.g., *"I must have done something wrong to deserve this"* or *"The world is not safe"*).

* If you are having frequent frightening thoughts or worries. Most women will experience distressing thoughts (including worries about something happening to their baby), but if these thoughts keep you from sleeping, make it hard to get through the day, or are causing frequent emotional distress, it could help to talk to someone.

* If you are dealing with frequent feelings of sadness, find it difficult to get up in the morning, notice you have lost your enjoyment in life, or have thoughts about harming yourself or others.

Finally, you do not have to give birth to experience the challenges of new parenthood. Dads and nonbirthing parents can also experience changes in mood after a child arrives. If you became a mom through surrogacy, adoption, or marriage, it is still important for you to take note of any of these symptoms.

A SELF-LOVE PRACTICE CAN HELP

Self-love really can help with the many challenges of being a mom. For example, imagine a tired first-time mom who is beating herself up after forgetting a doctor's appointment. She's feeling guilty, worried she won't get her child in for a checkup quickly enough, and afraid others will judge her.

Responding with self-love will start with acceptance. Remember, accepting something doesn't mean you approve of it. It's about noticing what is going on in a given moment (she forgot the appointment and is being self-critical) without trying to change reality (replaying the situation over and over and thinking about what "should" have happened).

If this mom can fully accept what happened, she will more quickly be able to stop spending energy wishing it hadn't happened or beating herself up. She can then treat herself as she might treat a friend, assuring herself it is an understandable mistake. She can offer herself some compassion and recognize she is feeling over-whelmed and tired. She may even be able to push herself to open up to her partner and ask for help because she knows she deserves support.

Loving Yourself Makes You a Better Parent

When we love ourselves, we believe in and trust ourselves. This is critical, since parenting so often requires consistency. Whether you are trying to help your new-born adjust to a new bath time routine or setting boundaries for a teenager, getting through these tasks requires stable execution time and time again. This becomes much easier when you have a strong sense of self-love. When the inevitable self-doubts arise, self-love will help you remember there is a reason you chose this path, and it will help you remain true to yourself and consistent with your child.

Loving Yourself Makes You a Better Role Model

The more self-love becomes part of your daily routine, the more you'll lead by example. Picture this: Instead of your child hearing you criticize your body, they see you take care of it. Even better, they see you celebrate it, with clothes that make you feel amazing (or amazingly comfortable). Or maybe you realize you forgot to do some-thing (even something important). Rather than seeing you use a choice four-letter word and put yourself down, they see you take a breath and make a note to help you remember for next time. Your self-love teaches them self-love.

Loving Yourself Helps You Feel Strong, Empowered, and Ready to Face Anything

The best way to get to where you want to go is to accept where you are right now. Imagine preparing to go back to work after maternity leave. You might feel like you should be able to hit the ground running. Instead, from a place of self-love, you prepare for your first day back knowing it may be emotional and overwhelming. Your loving self helps you set small, realistic goals for the day. Because of this, even though the day is challenging, you accomplish each of your goals. Now you feel better and more motivated for day two!

Loving Yourself Can Help with Day-to-Day Anxiety, Loneliness, Depression, and Stress

Self-love is a powerful tool to help you cope with these common day-to-day challenges. By working to celebrate yourself, recognizing and tending to your feelings, and offering yourself compassion when you struggle or mess up, you will reduce your overall suffering. This is because self-love doesn't require you to be perfect or to feel any specific way. Just as you might comfort a friend who is crying, self-love calls you to self-soothe, making space for difficult emotions to be present and allowing them to move on their way.

Quick Self-Love Hacks

Developing self-love requires daily practice. Following are three exercises to increase your love for your body, mind, and emotions. You can do these in less than a minute or take as long as you like.

* **Loving your body.** Wherever you are, stop and close your eyes. Quickly scan your body and notice where there is any tension. Bring your hands to cover any area of tension and gently rub or hold this part of your body. Try to notice the warmth your hands bring. Allow yourself two to three slow breaths as you thank your body for all the work it is doing for you and your family.

* **Loving your mind.** Close your eyes and take a moment to notice that no matter what, your mind is busy keeping you alive. It is keeping your lungs working and your heart beating, even if it forgot where you put your phone. See if you can take a moment to feel some appreciation for your mind and say, "I see you, brain. Thanks for all you do to keep me alive each day."

* **Loving your feelings.** Find a comfortable place to sit. Notice what you are feeling in this moment and try to name the feeling (sadness, anger, fear, happiness, etc.). Whether the feeling is painful or pleasant, say "thank you" to the emotion. Notice what it feels like to welcome and appreciate that feeling rather than trying to push it away.

LOVE YOURSELF THE WAY YOU LOVE YOUR CHILD

Think back to the last time your child really needed you. Maybe they needed something to eat, a diaper change, or a hug after a difficult day at school. In the time between when you realized your child needed something and the time you began tending to their needs, what did you do? While you may have stopped to consider how you would meet that need (like when you're in the bathroom and your toddler insists on a snack!), it's not likely you stopped to weigh your child's flaws and accomplishments before deciding if you would help them. You probably didn't ask if they worked hard enough to earn your love and comfort. No, chances are you offered your child love, compassion, respect, acceptance, and admiration every day. The trick now is to start doing this for yourself as well. Take time to meet your own needs, offer yourself comfort and support, and be kind to yourself in difficult moments. Love yourself the way you love your child; you both deserve that.

CONCLUSION

By now you may be starting to get a better sense of what self-love means. Developing self-love will help you see the beauty and power in who you are today and who you'll become as you continue your journey in life and parenthood, but it isn't enough to know what self-love is and why it's important. You'll need to take regular action to strengthen each domain of self-love: self-acceptance, self-compassion, and showing yourself respect and admiration. Chapter 2 will get you started with some concrete steps, including how to make time for yourself no matter how busy you are.

As a parent, if you give
yourself what you need,
your children will watch
you doing that and will give
themselves what they need.

—SUSAN CAIN

two.
HOW TO
GET STARTED

No matter how you became a mom, there are likely to be some struggles as you adjust to your new role. These challenges can set you up to focus on things you wish you had done differently and hold on to "what-ifs." In truth, no one does the mom thing perfectly. The more you can embrace your whole self, the more you will be able to make peace with where you have been and move forward in a valuable, meaningful way. This chapter will help you continue your self-love journey, suggesting ways to put self-love into action and sharing ideas to help you work through common barriers. Keep reading—you're on your way!

THERE'S NO ONE RIGHT WAY
TO PRACTICE SELF-LOVE

Like motherhood, learning to love yourself is an inherently personal practice; there's no one right way to do it. As a first-time mom, you are probably familiar with seeking advice or stumbling on parenting hacks promising easy fixes. Sometimes these tips work and sometimes they don't. That's okay! As you learn to love yourself more fully, be open to both learning new ways to care for yourself and feeling completely comfortable rejecting what doesn't work. I encourage you to apply this to your parenting as well. If another mom's suggestion doesn't work, consider Amy Poehler's motto for women: "Good for her! Not for me."

TAKE YOUR TIME TO FIGURE OUT WHAT YOU
ENJOY (AND WHAT YOU'LL MAKE TIME FOR)

The Internet is filled with advice on how to practice self-love. It's often offered by people with good intentions who wish to share what has worked for them. You have likely encountered some of this advice. Maybe it was helpful; maybe it wasn't. The problem is, when we try to love ourselves using the methods that work for others, we risk entering a frustrating cycle of trying something, finding it doesn't really help, and then judging ourselves as somehow defective for not being able to benefit from something that was successful for someone else. As you continue through this chapter, pay attention to how you feel as you try out different practices. Bookmark the ones you enjoy and that work for your life. Fit the practices into your life rather than the other way around to find success.

GET CLEAR ON THE SELF-LOVE
PRACTICES YOU PREFER

As you go through this book, you'll find many types of exercises designed to help improve each aspect of self-love. Some will help you accept all the unique parts of yourself, others will help you be gentle with yourself, and still others will remind you that you are worthy and deserve to celebrate achievements. These exercises will also come in different forms, including activities to do alone or with others, challenges, and ways to shift your thinking. As you move forward in this book, pay attention to what types of self-love practices you prefer, and start there.

A Bubble Bath

For many moms, even a shower can seem like an unattainable goal some days; however, you do need to get clean. If you are someone who finds baths relaxing, give yourself permission to schedule a full-on bubble bath. Talk to your partner or a friend who can help with childcare, and allow yourself to recharge.

A Bedtime Book

Sleep can be hard to come by as a first-time mom, and many common bedtime habits can negatively impact the quality of what little sleep you get. Time spent scrolling social media on your phone can increase feelings of anxiety, and the light from the screen can disrupt sleep. Instead, try keeping a fun, easy book by the bed. Reading a few pages may be enough to help you unwind and be ready to sleep, with the added benefit of helping you connect to an enjoyable activity. Bonus points for nonfiction or just-for-fun books!

A Breathing Meditation with Your Child

Your breath can be a powerful tool to center yourself and soothe painful emotions, but it takes practice. The good news? You have a wonderful little helper. Kids are great at natural and relaxed breathing. The next time your child is asleep, watch as their stomach rises and falls while they breathe. Begin to slow your own breath as you focus on them. Focus simply on breathing and allow your mind to rest. You may notice at first your mind wanders off—that's normal, just keep practicing!

A Yoga or Workout Class

Moving your body is another way to practice self-love. Exercise, in any form, gives you a chance to connect with yourself. Regular exercise also increases energy levels. As a first-time mom, it can be difficult to find the time, but even a 10- or 15-minute online class can give you a quick boost. Plus, done regularly, exercise gives you a chance to experience growth and change. You may notice yourself lengthening that

10-minute walk or stretching further in that yoga pose. These wins give you a chance to recognize your achievements.

Coffee with a Friend

Many first-time moms report feeling disconnected from their friends. You may feel this especially if you became a mom before your friends, or if they have children in a different stage than yours. Making time to reconnect, over a cup of coffee, tea, a meal, or a park bench, honors that need for connection and tends to any feelings of loneliness you may be having.

A Nap

While the constant advice to "sleep when the baby sleeps" can feel tiresome, sleep is a critical part of your mental and physical health. When we don't sleep enough, our emotions can feel more overwhelming. Author and researcher Sara Mednick, PhD, studies the benefits of naps. Her research shows naps of just 15 to 20 minutes can help you feel more alert. These short naps can be a great way to show yourself some care, especially when things are hectic.

HOW DO YOU MAKE TIME FOR SELF-LOVE?

So how do you find time to actually work on this self-love thing? In some ways, the answer to that is unique to each person. Some moms enjoy waking up extra early to have time to themselves before their children are awake; others stay up late and relish their evenings. Still other moms don't like either of these options or have kids with a supernatural ability to know when Mom is up. The good news is you don't need lots of time, money, or other tools to develop self-love. Finding some time for yourself can be helpful, but it's not required.

Remember in chapter 1 we defined self-love as accepting all the unique parts of yourself, being gentle with yourself, believing you are worthy, and recognizing your achievements, big and small. A big part of this is listening less to your inner critic and speaking to yourself more gently. For example, you might say to yourself, "Kristen will understand I am running late" instead of "I'm such a mess. Why can't I ever be on time?" These small actions can add up and help improve your self-love.

Acknowledge Taking Time for Yourself Is Hard

With all the challenges of being a first-time mom, it's easy to see why self-love might not always feel like a priority. Allow yourself to build your self-love practice slowly. Acknowledge this is hard work and give yourself credit for small wins. By doing this, you are already practicing self-love!

Your Child Wants a Happy Mom

Many first-time moms report feeling selfish or lazy when they take time to care for themselves. This is understandable given the pressure many new moms feel from society, their family, and themselves, but learning to truly love and embrace yourself does not come at the expense of your child. In fact, having a mom who is healthy and happy will benefit them. By making time for yourself, you give them the opportunity to learn from your healthy habits.

PUT IT IN YOUR CALENDAR

According to the research of psychologists Edwin Locke and Gary Latham, when we make a concrete plan to do something, we are more likely to follow through. Taking the time to decide when, where, and how you will show up for yourself helps you problem-solve obstacles and keeps you accountable.

One way to do this is to use your calendar. I encourage people to put two types of self-love events in their calendar. The first is daily reminders. As you work through this book, you will find many options for quick daily practices (self-affirmation, brief gratitude practices, and more). Many of these can be done anywhere and take just a few seconds. So put some reminders in your calendar to help you practice consistently.

The second type of event is scheduling actual time for yourself. This could be anything from a nap to coffee with a friend. If you have a shared calendar with your partner, put this time there. This will help ensure your partner is ready to be the parent on duty.

ASK FOR HELP FROM YOUR SUPPORT TEAM

Being a first-time mom can really take a lot out of you. Surviving is much easier if you have a support team—and if you let yourself ask them for help. This last part is hard. Asking for help can make you feel vulnerable. This is especially true for moms who often feel they should be able to keep up and do things on their own.

No matter what obstacles are in your way, I encourage you to take the risk and ask for help. Help is great for you! When others help you out, you get back some of your much-needed time and energy. That's a huge win. Even better, helping is great for those around you. Many of the people in your life want to help; they just don't know how. Asking gives your loved ones an opportunity to show you they care. You also allow them to feel needed and trusted.

Your Partner, Friends, and Family

Once you decide to start asking for help, you'll need to consider how best to do it. While it can be tempting to believe those closest to you "should" know what you want or need from them, this is an unhelpful assumption that can lead to resentment and pain. Making a clear request is the best course of action. Requests for help ("Can you wash the dishes?") and for support ("Can we meet up for lunch? I need a fun distraction.") have a better chance of being met when they are clear.

Reach Out to Your Wider Support Network

Think about your broader network. Chances are you have a number of people in your life who are full of knowledge and helpful information. That woman at work whose kid is two years older than yours is probably full of useful tips; maybe she can help you navigate company policy to create a more flexible schedule so you can manage morning drop-off. If you start thinking creatively, you may find there are many people who can help you pick a gym, cover your inbox while you leave early for the day, or recommend a reliable babysitter.

Three Ways to Involve Your Child in Your Self-Love Practice

1. **Sing/dance-along.** Create a playlist of songs for feeling hopeful, energized, and happy. The next time you need a boost of energy, take a step back from the situation and pick one song and commit to dancing or singing with your child.

2. **Savor the good.** First-time moms tend to worry about being "good enough." The next time you have a calm moment, take a beat to really watch your child and look for evidence of all the things you are doing right. Notice the cute laugh when they feel happy and secure, the way your arms so often seem to comfort them, or when they are studying quietly thanks to your support of their schoolwork. Whatever it may be, notice the good and give yourself some credit.

3. **Meditate together.** Meditation and yoga practices are great for children. Many meditation apps have prompts specifically geared toward children. Why not do these together? This way both you and your child are learning to take time for yourselves, together.

HOW OFTEN SHOULD YOU PRACTICE SELF-LOVE?

How often should you practice self-love? There is no one answer. Some things, like sleeping, eating, and moving your body, are best done daily. These physical needs impact your physical and emotional health; however, it can be hard for first-time moms to meet them, especially if you have an infant. It is an act of self-love to believe you are worthy of the time and support from others to get these needs met. If you are struggling in this area, reach out to your support team.

How often you need to practice in other areas, like self-acceptance, self-compassion, and recognizing your achievements, can vary from person to person. Once you master these skills, you will start to do them naturally in your daily life. You will be acting with self-love and may not need to intentionally practice as frequently.

For example, if you feel pretty comfortable in your own body, meaning you know and accept its imperfections and have an overall positive relationship with your body, then you may only need to intentionally work on your body image when something triggers an insecurity (body changes from pregnancy, for example). If, however, you tend to struggle with body image, daily and intentional practices can help you develop a healthier outlook.

Five Minutes Is Better Than Nothing

As you see, self-love can take many forms. If you are new to this, or if you have really lost touch with your ability to love yourself, then start slowly and steadily. It can be tempting to take on everything at once, but I encourage you to pick one area of self-love to focus on. Work to build a sustainable daily routine. Start with just five minutes and build from there.

A Consistent Practice Will Be More Rewarding

Consistency is key when you are trying to build new patterns. For this reason, taking small steps daily leads to more lasting and rewarding change. For example, you know that inner voice that downplays your accomplishments and tells you it is selfish to take care of yourself? That voice is with you each day. You need to counter these messages of self-judgment and doubt daily for your inner messages of love and acceptance to become louder.

LIFE GETS BUSY—FORGIVE YOURSELF IF YOU FORGET

Truly loving yourself does not require perfection. Some days and weeks you will be able to stick to your plans, showing yourself love in all the ways you need. Other times you may feel like you're drowning, and all the skills you've developed will slip right out of your mind. This is part of being human.

You are doing the best you can each day, given your circumstances. Your best today will be different from your best tomorrow, next week, or last year. That is okay. So what does this mean for you? Well, I hope reflecting on this reminds you to be kind to yourself and practice self-love. As a first-time mom, you are learning so much and developing new skills as you adjust. You can't remember everything all the time!

BE GENTLE WITH YOURSELF

Moving through your life with self-love doesn't require you to always be able to sleep well, move your body, see your friends, or engage in other time-consuming activities. In fact, one of the most common ways people damage their self-love is by holding themselves up to some list of unattainable standards. Rather than beating yourself up for not taking care of yourself, see if you can be gentle. Thank your inner critic for reminding you your needs are important. Then offer yourself some kind words, thanking your body for all the other work it has been doing. Noticing what you have been doing, rather than focusing on what you have forgotten, is an act of self-love. You are already back on track.

SET SMALL GOALS EACH DAY

As you work on the skills and practices in this book, you will begin to see important shifts in yourself. Some of these shifts will be small—you may notice you don't criticize yourself as harshly for that spilled coffee or for feeling angry with your toddler. Some changes will seem larger; you may notice yourself setting aside "you" time each day and getting better at asking your network for help. You may also simply start feeling more comfortable with yourself, no longer focusing on what you should do differently. To create these changes, regular practice is key. Set one small goal for yourself each day—maybe it's doing one exercise from this book. Start small, stay consistent, and big changes will happen.

YOU'RE READY TO START

So much is possible when we really learn to love ourselves. Truly knowing you are worthy of care and time, learning to be kind to yourself, and learning to accept your flaws, knowing you can continue to grow, will help you be the best version of yourself. At this point in your journey, and almost two chapters into this workbook, I hope you are beginning to recognize the truth in these statements. If not, it's okay. You are allowed to feel a bit skeptical. You may even feel overwhelmed at the prospect of adding one more thing to your plate. It is true that self-love means trying new things and putting time and energy into yourself, even if you feel you don't have much to give. Feeling doubtful is normal. As long as you are willing to keep an open mind and try out the suggestions in this workbook, you are ready to begin!

Quiz/Assessment:
Self-Love Status

You're almost ready to begin part 2 of this book. Before you do, take a moment to reflect on where you are now. Read each of the questions and indicate on a scale of 1 to 5 how much you agree with each statement.

1 = Strongly disagree, **2** = Disagree, **3** = Undecided,
4 = Agree, **5** = Strongly agree

1. I do not believe I deserve love and support from others.

    1   2   3   4   5

2. I would not talk to others the way I talk to myself.

    1   2   3   4   5

3. I focus more on my failures as a parent than I do on the ways I am succeeding.

    1   2   3   4   5

4. I feel selfish when I try to take care of my own needs.

    1   2   3   4   5

5. I have a hard time telling others no.

    1   2   3   4   5

6. I try to avoid looking in the mirror, and when I do, I focus on my flaws.

    1   2   3   4   5

7. I struggle to ask for help, even from my partner and close friends.

    1   2   3   4   5

8. I am not sure I deserve help.

    1   2   3   4   5

9. I often think I am a "bad mom" and take any challenges or negative
    behaviors my child displays as proof of my failures.

    1   2   3   4   5

10. I have a hard time accepting a compliment with a simple "thank
    you." Instead, I tend to minimize it or point out my flaws.

    1   2   3   4   5

SCORING:

0 to 10: Really nice work! Keep it up and you will build an even
stronger sense of love and self-compassion, which will help you
throughout your personal and parenting journey.

11 to 30: You have a good foundation, though you struggle at times
to accept yourself and can be a harsh self-critic. Keep moving through
this book and take time to complete the practices that speak to you.

31 to 50: You are focusing much of your attention on your perceived
flaws and inadequacies. You may feel this will motivate you to change
or do better, but it doesn't work that way. You are an amazing person
and deserve to fully embrace yourself, flaws and all. Keep working
through this book to learn more about developing self-love and
why self-love, not self-criticism, will help you become the mom you
truly want to be.

CONCLUSION

I hope by now you are getting a better sense of all the ways you can practice self-love, both through your actions and in your thoughts. As you keep working, it's important to remember little humans have an outsize ability to throw our days into chaos. As a first-time mom, you will be learning more and more with each new stage your child reaches, and this means your self-love routine and practices may need to change over time. In the next section, you will find a mix of ideas. Some take less than a minute. Some you should do on your own, and others can be done with your child. Not every exercise will feel right for you, but I hope some will resonate and help you forward on your path.

Be gentle first with yourself if you wish to be gentle with others.

—LAMA YESHE

PART TWO

SHOW YOURSELF LOVE

Welcome to part 2! Unlike part 1, where I did most of the talking, in part 2 you will be the star of the show. I will still be here to guide you, but your writing, thoughts, and actions will be what matter most. In part 2, each chapter will focus on different areas of self-love and provide useful examples, strategies, and exercises to guide you as you strengthen your self-love. It may be difficult to get motivated to try different exercises, and writing down your thoughts can make you feel vulnerable, but take a chance, despite your fears and doubts. You deserve it.

You are allowed to heal
toward a future version
of yourself without hating
who you are right now.
You have the option to
love yourself to new levels.

—RACHEL ELIZABETH CARGLE

· three.

EMBRACE YOURSELF, FLAWS AND ALL

Accepting all the unique parts of yourself is critical for self-love. It is also difficult, especially when you are focused on your flaws or struggling to find your balance between your old self and your new identity as a mom.

The best way to start reaching your goals and building the life you want is to really notice where you are right now, no matter how fulfilled you feel or how far you still need to go. In this chapter, you will work through a range of exercises that will help you connect to yourself, begin to clarify your current goals, and reduce self-judgment, freeing you to embrace your whole self.

IDENTIFY YOUR GOALS

The upcoming chapters will be filled with exercises and useful information designed to help you increase your self-love. Before you begin, it will be helpful to set some concrete goals for yourself as you move forward in this workbook.

1. What am I hoping to gain from my work in this book?

Ex: more self-confidence, feeling more at peace, better self-care habits

_____

_____

2. How will I put what I learn into practice?

Ex: I will complete one exercise a day or I will spend 10 minutes each day on self-love.

_____

_____

3. What will be different when I reach my goals?

Ex: I will be able to ask for help from others.

_____

_____

4. What will get in the way of reaching my goals?

Ex: time, energy, or fear of being successful

_____

_____

5. What steps can I take to overcome these barriers?

Ex: enlisting my support system

_____

_____

EXPLORE WHERE YOU ARE

It's important to make sense of any physical and emotional changes as you build your new identity as a first-time mom. Following is a three-part exercise to help you visualize and reflect on some of those changes.

Step 1: Take a moment to reflect on all the things that made you who you were in your pre-baby life. These could be your hobbies, your work, your friendships, anything that made you *you*. Then divide up the pie, creating slices that represent each of those parts. The slices can be as big or small as you need; the goal is to reflect how important those parts of your identity were to you before you had your child.

Step 2: Repeat that process for your life now, as a mother.

Step 3: Take a look at the two images you created. What do you notice? How have things changed? How do you feel about those changes? In the space provided, write about what you are noticing. If you find there are things about the second pie you want to change, like making a slice bigger or eliminating a slice, that's okay. Include this in your writing. It's important to recognize and embrace where you are today.

_____

_____

_____

_____

_____

KNOW WHAT MATTERS

Part of fully embracing yourself is knowing what goals and values matter to you. Goals are what you want to accomplish; they're the destination. Values are the path you take to get there. They're what's important to you in *how* you live your life. Knowing your values and acting accordingly can increase your sense of satisfaction in life, even when you are struggling to meet a goal or adjusting to a major life change.

Consider some of the roles you play in your daily life. In the space provided, reflect on how you want to show up in these roles. What values do you want to live by? Some examples of values are caring, creative, honest, funny, hardworking, strong, generous, passionate, or loyal.

As a mother, I want to be . . .

As a partner, I want to be . . .

As a friend, I want to be . . .

As a _____,
I want to be . . .

ACT ON WHAT MATTERS

Reflect on the values you wrote down in the previous exercise. Now consider how well you are living by those values. Pick one and take a moment to think about things you currently do that move you away from that value, as well as actions you can take to move toward it. Write those in the space that follows.

Actions away from my values

_____

_____

_____

_____

_____

_____

_____

Actions toward my values

_____

_____

_____

_____

_____

_____

_____

This week, focus on moving toward your values. Repeat the exercise with as many life roles (friend, mother, partner, etc.) as you want.

NOTICE WHERE YOUR TIME GOES

Spend five minutes reflecting on your daily activities (work, vacuuming, sleep training, etc.). If you couldn't do these things tomorrow, which activities would you really miss because they are important, and what, if left undone, would mostly worry you due to fears of being judged?

What really matters to me

_____

_____

_____

_____

_____

_____

_____

_____

_____

What I worry others will judge me for

_____

_____

_____

_____

_____

_____

_____

_____

_____

Now take a look at these two lists. How are they the same? How are they different? It is completely understandable if you worry others may judge you; this is a normal human reaction. However, by breaking down these lists and knowing where they differ, you can think more critically about the items on the "judge me" list. If you are spending your time worrying about judgment, experiment with focusing more of your energy on what matters to you. What does that feel like?

WHAT IS ACCEPTANCE?

One main barrier to acceptance is misunderstanding what it means. Acceptance of yourself, your flaws, or what happens in your life isn't the same as approving of those things. When you accept, you are not surrendering, and you are not saying that your circumstances won't change. Acceptance is really just about letting go of our attempts to change the past or things that are beyond our control.

For example, as a first-time mom you may be struggling to accept that you need to feed your baby formula because your body isn't producing enough breastmilk. If breastfeeding is important to you, this may be a really painful reality, but criticizing your body or judging yourself won't increase your milk supply. Acceptance here means taking the steps you need to care for your child while also being kind to yourself and letting go of the judgment and blame that gets in the way of self-love.

ACCEPTANCE TRIFECTA: THREE STEPS TO EMBRACE LIFE AS IT IS

Here are three steps you can take when you find yourself struggling to accept something happening in your life.

Step 1: Pay Attention to Your Thoughts. A helpful way to catch yourself rejecting rather than embracing reality is to pay attention to any thoughts about what "should" or "shouldn't" be happening. Maybe you think "I shouldn't be angry" or "My partner should do more." Take a moment to notice that you are trying to reject what is happening, and jot down what you are pushing away:

_____

_____

_____

Step 2: Notice What Is. Pick one of the preceding items and try to rewrite it without the "should," so you are simply describing what is:

Ex: I should be able to do this. → I feel overwhelmed and tired.

_____

_____

Step 3: Embrace Where You Are. Sit in a comfortable position and read over the sentence you came up with in step 2. As you do, notice what feelings and thoughts come up for you.

Rather than returning to the place of should or shouldn't, see if you can allow whatever comes up to be there.

Once you can sit with your reactions, you can respond gently and with kindness. If you feel sad, try to comfort yourself. If you feel angry, notice what you need. Now that you have embraced life as it is, you can respond to it, rather than wishing for it to be different.

LETTING GO OF CONTROL

So often moms get stuck criticizing themselves ("I'm a terrible mom. I let my kid have too much screen time") or worrying about things out of their control ("Will kids at school be nice today?"). It's tempting to believe being the "right" kind of mom will ensure your child is successful or that if you work hard enough, you're guaranteed to reach your goals. The truth is we only have control over our own actions, and even that can be a struggle. In each cloud, write one thing you are worried about. Put a circle around the ones you can control and place an X on the ones you can't control.

Now focus your energy on the worries you can control.

YOU ARE NOT ALONE

Many first-time moms feel like they aren't good enough. It can feel like you are alone in your worries or seem like your thoughts are evidence that something is wrong. That is not true. Following are some common first-time mom struggles. Circle what you've experienced.

Was becoming a mom a mistake? Maybe I'm not cut out for this.

That woman in the mirror doesn't even look like me.

What happened to my body?

I don't feel like myself anymore.

Why can't I make a decision?

I feel exhausted.

What if I drop the baby?

Why am I crying?

I don't want to be touched.

I'm so scared all the time.

No one even asks about me; it's like I don't even matter to them anymore.

Everyone else seems to have it together. What's wrong with me?

Next time you notice one of these thoughts, remind yourself you are not alone; you are in the good company of other amazing first-time moms. Rather than pushing away the thought, try to allow it to exist. Remember, a thought is not proof of anything. If you need to, take a moment to refocus your attention on something calming—the bright sun outside, the soft feel of a blanket, the sweet smell of your child (even if they are crying).

EMBRACE THAT FEELING! YES, EVEN THAT ONE

All people experience painful feelings, and it is common to want to push away these feelings. This is especially true for first-time moms who feel they need to keep it together to take care of everyone else. The trouble is those feelings are telling you something important. The next time you have strong feelings, try noticing what they want you to do. Remember, you don't always need to do what your feelings are telling you, but by listening, you can actively choose how you want to respond.

Feeling	What the feeling is communicating	What the feeling tells me to do
Ex: Sadness	I'm lonely and miss time with friends	Cry, seek comfort

ALLOWING EMOTION

Next time you find yourself caught up in painful emotions following a difficult moment with your child, take five minutes to follow these steps.

1. Find a comfortable place to sit.

2. Take several slow breaths, allowing yourself to relax into your chair.

3. Bring the difficult moment to mind.

4. See if you can name the emotion(s): "I am feeling frustrated." "I am feeling sad."

5. Sit with that emotion, feeling it rather than resisting it or trying to get away from it.

6. Notice where that feeling is in your body.

7. Notice if the feeling has any color, shape, or movement.

8. Notice if the feeling is pulling you to do anything (escape, yell, cry).

9. Be as curious as you can about the emotion, allowing it to be with you.

10. As you allow yourself to connect with this feeling, repeat this thought to yourself: "I can be a good mom and feel all my feelings."

RECOGNIZING JUDGMENT

Learning to embrace yourself means learning to speak to yourself from a place of compassion. Following is a list of common phrases I hear from first-time moms who are hard on themselves. The words in red show up frequently when we are judging ourselves or others. Circle the words or phrases that you feel you are most prone to use.

I **can't** take it **anymore.**

I **never** do anything **right.**

This is all just **too** much.

That person must think I'm a **horrible** mother.

She **always** looks **perfect.**

I **should** be able to do this.

I'm **such a mess.**

These words are your personal red flags; they signal that you may have moved out of self-love. When this happens, take a brief pause and see if you can describe what is happening around you without the judgment words. Once you start doing this, you may find your emotions shift slightly. You may even be able to think of ways to solve the problem.

Ex: I never do anything right → I went to work with spit-up on my clothes and feel embarrassed.

Each mistake I make is a chance
to love myself more fully.

WOW! YOU DID SO MUCH TODAY!

I'm willing to bet that you, as a first-time mom, have days when you judge yourself because you "didn't get enough done." On days like this, you have probably been doing so much more than you realize.

Here is a list of things you might have done today. Check the things you did and add your own. Your list will look different depending on whether you are working outside the home, tending to an infant, or running after a toddler. No matter what you did, you did *so much*.

☐ Kept a tiny human alive

☐ Managed my own emotions

☐ Made it out of bed despite getting almost no sleep

☐ Fed myself and those depending on me

☐ Comforted a friend

☐ Soothed my child

☐ Responded to/checked email

☐ _____

☐ _____

☐ _____

☐ _____

☐ _____

☐ _____

☐ _____

☐ _____

☐ _____

☐ _____

FLIP YOUR FLAWS

Very often, the things we judge about ourselves have a good reason for being. For example, that postpartum body you're unhappy with made your child. Those scary thoughts running through your head, while unhelpful, are a sign your brain is trying to protect you from danger. In the following chart, write some things about yourself you perceive as flaws, then see if you can flip them.

Flaw	Positive meaning
Ex: I worry constantly.	I care deeply about the safety and well-being of my family.
Ex: I'm a terrible cook.	My not cooking allows my partner to feel like a vital part of our family with an important job to do, and I care for myself and our family in other ways.

CREATE YOUR ACCEPTANCE MANTRA

Finding a mantra you can use when you are being self-critical can help shift your thinking. Some examples are listed here, but I encourage you to write what feels authentic. Practice using the mantra daily.

Ex:

Perfection is not required of me.

I am doing the best I can in this moment.

I am still a good mom if _____.

I can feel anger/doubt/sadness and still love my child.

My thoughts and feelings don't define me.

Today, I am amazing just the way I am.

_____

_____

_____

_____

_____

_____

_____

_____

_____

_____

_____

_____

_____

_____

TAKE STOCK OF YOUR SKILLS

Answer the following questions:

What are some things others do better than you?

_____

_____

_____

What are some things you are just average at?

_____

_____

_____

What are some things you do well or better than most?

_____

_____

_____

When you're done, take a moment to look at these lists. It's important to remember you don't have to be good at something to enjoy doing it. Try to embrace yourself fully, both for what you do well and what you don't.

Pro tip: If you have a hard time with the lists, ask your partner or friends for help.

SOMEONE TO LEAN ON

Feelings of guilt or shame over something we have said, done, or experienced can make us withdraw or hide parts of ourselves from the people closest to us. This pattern leaves many first-time moms feeling alone. Sure, you can read online about the many struggles of being a mom, but it isn't the same as being able to talk to someone you trust about what you are going through.

When we embrace ourselves fully and open up to others, it can help in so many ways.

* Sharing your successes with others lets you feel proud of what you have accomplished and brings you support and encouragement from others.

* When you share painful feelings and thoughts with others, you can receive care and compassion from them. While sharing can make you feel vulnerable, it is a way to honor your emotions and needs. Perhaps even more importantly, it deepens your relationships with people close to you.

* When we share things we don't like about ourselves, including mistakes we've made or thoughts we feel ashamed of, we bring these things to light. In doing so, we often find out that others have experienced similar situations, and even if they haven't, they often want to offer support rather than judgment.

Over the next week, practice sharing the highs and lows of your day-to-day with someone close to you. Notice how your feelings change when you share them with others.

CONCLUSION

I hope you feel you have made some progress toward accepting your whole self, including your emotions, worries, thoughts, and flaws. As you move forward, remember you can return to these practices and exercises whenever you need to. Learning to embrace yourself is not a one-time thing; it is something we all must work on over time. This is especially true for first-time moms—you will continue to make mistakes, learn, and change as your child grows! Next, we'll explore the importance of embracing and accepting your body just as it is today.

Accepting yourself
only as long as you look a
certain way isn't self-love,
it's self-destruction.

—LACI GREEN

four.

CHERISH YOUR BODY

This chapter isn't called "Love Your Body." While the goal of this book is to help you learn to love yourself more, loving your body is not required. In fact, it's a high bar to clear for most of us. Believing that we have to love our bodies in order to be content with them sets us up to fail.

In truth, most people with a positive body image don't have strong feelings of love for every part of themselves. Instead, people who feel good about their bodies tend to know their physical appearance is just one aspect of who they are and what their body is capable of. This chapter will guide you through prompts and exercises to help you better understand your current relationship with your body and build a stronger and healthier relationship with it.

BEGIN WITH GRATITUDE

No matter what path you took to motherhood, becoming a mom is a full-body experience. Take a moment to shift your attention away from any perceived flaws and appreciate all the hard work your body has done for you and your family. Reflect on what your body has accomplished on this journey, and then use the space to write a thank-you letter to your body.

Dear Body,

_____

_____

_____

_____

_____

_____

_____

_____

_____

_____

_____

_____

_____

_____

_____

_____

_____

_____

UNDERSTANDING YOUR BODY IMAGE

Psychologist Joel Kevin Thompson has suggested body image contains three elements: your mental image of yourself, your thoughts and feelings about this mental picture, and your actions in response to these thoughts and emotions.

The first graphic shows these elements working together in a negative cycle. See if you can fill in the blanks with positive alternatives.

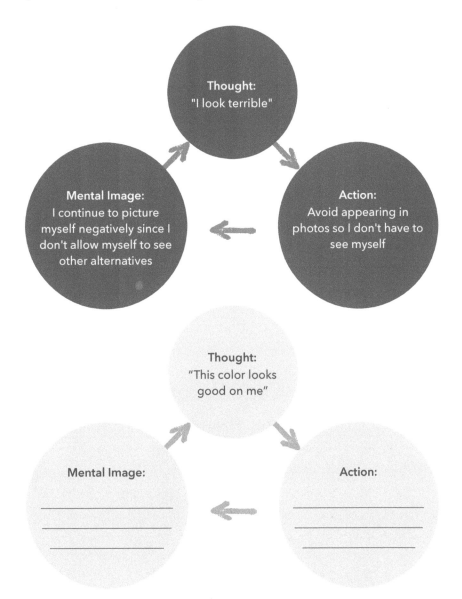

QUIZ: ARE YOU AVOIDING YOUR BODY?

Check the box for the answer that feels most accurate for you.

	Yes	No
1. I make efforts to wear loose or baggy clothes to hide my body.	☐	☐
2. I won't let people take photos of me with my child because I don't want to look at myself.	☐	☐
3. I don't leave home without make-up on.	☐	☐
4. I avoid looking at myself in the mirror.	☐	☐
5. I avoid getting on the scale at doctor's appointments.	☐	☐
6. I try to avoid spending time with people who will comment on my appearance.	☐	☐
7. I try to avoid situations where I will be around people who I think are attractive or stylish.	☐	☐
8. I don't allow others to see me exercise or dance.	☐	☐
9. When I am around other people, I try to hide areas of my body using my hand or purse, or by holding my child.	☐	☐
10. I try to avoid thinking about my body or appearance whenever possible.	☐	☐

SCORING:

Give yourself 10 points for each question you answered with a yes.

0 to 40: You may occasionally avoid thinking about your appearance, but overall you are comfortable with your body whether you feel great or insecure. Keep up the good work.

50 to 100: You work hard to avoid connecting with your body. You may feel insecure and uncomfortable with your body in the present moment. Remember the three components of body image—when you avoid your body, it feeds the negative cycle. Keep working through this book to learn to let go of avoidance and embrace your body.

WHY AVOIDING YOUR BODY DOESN'T HELP

Because it can be painful to be reminded of our appearance, especially when feeling insecure, avoiding our bodies feels like a useful way to cope. Unfortunately, avoidance has the nasty habit of making you feel worse over time. When you avoid your body, it's difficult to connect to the positive things about it, robbing you of opportunities to feel good about yourself. It also teaches your brain some pretty unhelpful lessons.

Take, for example, the new mom who wants to avoid getting on a scale at the doctor's office. She begins to feel anxious and asks to not be told her weight—and the nurse agrees. She may feel relief for a moment but may also begin to notice anxious thoughts like, "What was that look on the nurse's face?" or "He thinks I weigh too much." This mom may even have a number in her head of how much she is afraid she weighs. These thoughts create more anxiety and can make it even harder the next time she needs to get on a scale. Instead, she could have used some of the skills in this chapter to remind herself that her weight is only one thing about her, making it easier to get on the scale and move forward with her day.

NOTICE CHANGE

In the space provided, rate how positively you felt about your body during different times in your life. Some sections may not apply to you; just skip over those.

1 = I don't like my body at all.   5 = I totally love my body!

High school

1   2   3   4   5

Adult life before baby

1   2   3   4   5

Pregnancy

1   2   3   4   5

While breastfeeding

1   2   3   4   5

1 to 12 months postpartum

1   2   3   4   5

1+ year(s) postpartum

1   2   3   4   5

Something else: _____

1   2   3   4   5

Take a moment to reflect on this. Do your numbers change over time? If so, that is great news! Regardless of how your feelings have changed, it's important to notice that feelings about your body do change. This means they can change for the better.

Many people find they feel best about their body during pregnancy. After pregnancy, many women feel pressure to return to "normal," which causes discomfort with the ways pregnancy has changed their body. If this is the case for you, you may notice that your more recent ratings are lower.

If your ratings are higher now, congratulations! Keep up the great work of appreciating your body as it is. Should you notice that your feelings toward your body change over time, you can always return to these exercises to help you reconnect with and appreciate your body.

MAKE A PLAN TO MOVE YOUR BODY

Moving your body is another important part of self-love. Not only does physical movement have a strong impact on your mental health, leading to reduced stress and improved sleep and mood, it can also positively impact how you feel about your body. When you move your body in healthy ways, you feel more connected to yourself and recognize what your body is capable of. Follow the steps to create your own plan to get moving.

Step 1: Find a way to move your body that you really enjoy, not something you do just because you think it's healthy. You can choose from the options provided or write in your own. Place a check mark by the ones you are willing to try:

- Yoga
- Stretching
- Walking
- Gardening

- Riding a bike
- Dancing
- _____
- _____

Step 2: Set a small goal. Even just 10 minutes a day can help you build a habit. What goal can you start with?

_____

_____

Step 3: Mark your progress. Noticing small changes over time will help keep you motivated. Try to stay away from weight loss–related goals, but find a way to track progress that feels meaningful for you. This can be the amount of time you spend moving in a week or the number of new poses you can do.

You can also rate your feelings about your body each week. Use a 0 to 10 scale, with 0 meaning you have only negative thoughts about your body and want it to change and 10 indicating that you fully embrace your body and view it as strong and capable.

Use the space on page 58 to make note of your progress for the next four weeks.

Week 1

Week 2

Week 3

Week 4

MOVEMENT EXPERIMENT

A lack of motivation is one common barrier to increasing movement and exercise. Sure, you have 15 minutes, but sitting on the couch can sound more appealing than doing a quick workout. The trouble is when we give in to scrolling on our phone or watching TV, we don't get much benefit. Moving your body can actually help reduce anxiety and stress and leave you feeling more energized or in a better mood. Don't believe me? Gather some data for yourself. Over the next few days, try out some of these activities and take note of how you feel before and after. See for yourself what works for you.

Activity	Mood before	Mood after
Workout class	_____	_____
Yoga	_____	_____
Walking	_____	_____
Jogging/running	_____	_____
Watching TV	_____	_____
Social media	_____	_____

THE BODY OF A MOTHER

Regardless of how you became a mother, nurturing a child can change your relationship with your body. Consider some of the ways your body is already different—dark circles from lack of sleep, a scar from a C-section, a bruise on your knee from bumping into something after a late-night feeding—then connect that change to something positive motherhood has given you.

Changes to my body

Ex: I feel less fit, as I had less time for exercise while adopting my child.

_____

_____

_____

_____

_____

_____

_____

_____

_____

_____

_____

_____

_____

What they have given me

More motivation to take long walks with my child each day so we both get to move.

_____

_____

_____

_____

_____

_____

_____

_____

_____

_____

_____

_____

_____

WHAT ARE YOUR BODY IMAGE RULES?

Take some time to think about your personal body and appearance rules (some examples are listed), and then think about where these rules come from. Once you recognize your rules and why you have them, you can make more mindful decisions about when and if to follow them.

As a first-time mom, you may already be breaking your own rules because you don't have the time or energy to follow them. This can actually increase your dissatisfaction with your body, so now that you know what your rules are, give yourself permission to break them (or follow them!) if you choose to.

Rule	Why I follow it
Ex: I can't wear shorts.	I feel self-conscious about my legs.
Ex: I put on make-up first thing.	I hate looking at myself without make-up on.

EMBRACE THAT PHOTO

If you tend to use avoidance to deal with a negative body image, you may find that taking pictures is a struggle. While you may think avoiding pictures is harmless, it means you are taking yourself out of the photo record of your child's life. There is another way! It takes practice, but you can get comfortable in front of the camera.

Step 1: When you look at a picture of yourself, notice what thoughts come to mind. If they are critical, that's okay; don't put the photo away. Instead, remind yourself that you are likely being overly critical of yourself and/or only focusing on one part of the overall picture.

Step 2: Remind yourself that this photo doesn't represent how you look; it is only one angle of a moment in time. Anyone can take a not-so-great photo.

Step 3: Expand your focus from just you to the larger picture. Try to notice what is going on and connect to the fun memories.

> I am allowed to feel good and
> take care of my body no matter
> what it looks like or how it changes.

COMPLIMENT BINGO

Both giving and receiving compliments can be difficult if you struggle with self-love. While you don't control if/when others compliment you, you can practice giving more compliments, especially ones that are not appearance-related. This is good practice for you and creates a healthy model for your children. Following is a bingo card filled with great compliments to give the adults and kids in your life. See if you can make it a point to get a bingo this week. How does it feel to compliment others on attributes besides their body?

That was a great idea!	You tell the best stories!	You have such great taste!	I appreciate how supportive you are.	You have such a calming presence.
You are a great listener.	You are such a quick learner.	I love the color of your shirt.	I always have a great time with you.	You are a great big sibling.
I admire how organized you are.	You did a great job following directions today.	FREE	You have a lovely singing voice.	You are a great artist.
Your smile makes me want to smile.	You are a wonderful friend.	I really feel I can trust you.	You are so brave.	I am so impressed with how well-read you are.
Working with you always helps me stay on task.	You are so funny!	I admire your creativity.	You are a wonderful mother!	You are such a great helper.

THE CLOSET CLEANUP

Do you ever step into your closet and become immediately disheartened? Maybe you look around and realize your clothes either don't fit or are so worn out that you feel like a mess when you wear them. This is a recipe for feeling unattractive. You deserve to have clothes in your closet that fit you and help you feel good about yourself.

Step 1: Pack up clothes that no longer fit you. Be honest with yourself about what is realistic to keep. Sure, if you recently gave birth, your body is still changing, and you may fit into some of your old clothes again. Keep those items somewhere where they will be organized and accessible but won't taunt you. Give the rest away.

Step 2: When you find a new item of clothing you like, give yourself permission to buy it, but in your current size. Don't add new clothes you can't comfortably wear, but do allow yourself to look and feel good in your body as it is today.

QUIZ: ARE YOU CHASING A DIFFERENT BODY?

To understand if this is something you do, answer each statement by circling the number that applies to you.

0 = Never   1 = Rarely   2 = Sometimes   3 = Frequently   4 = Most often   5 = Always

1. I am often on a diet.

    0   1   2   3   4   5

2. I follow a complex beauty and skin care routine.

    0   1   2   3   4   5

3. I have strict rules and/or expectations about my exercise schedule.

    0   1   2   3   4   5

4. I am willing to spend a lot of my money/time/energy for new products that help me cover flaws in my appearance.

    0   1   2   3   4   5

5. I take precautions to protect my appearance and prevent aging.

    0   1   2   3   4   5

SCORING:

Look over your responses and notice what numbers you tend to select. There really aren't right or wrong responses here, and it is worth your time to consider how you feel about each one. The more we chase after a certain look (higher numbers = more chasing), the more we reinforce the idea that our value depends on our appearance. People who chase also tend to overestimate how much their appearance is the cause of positive events in their life, which again reinforces more chasing.

REBUILD YOUR CONFIDENCE

Step 1: Whether you have always struggled with body image or are having trouble accepting your new-mom body, your body image may be impacting your behavior. Reflect on this for a moment. What don't you do because you worry you would feel insecure or be judged for your body?

Ex:

Take pictures of myself

Wear certain styles of clothing

Shop for new clothes that fit me (I'm waiting until I lose the baby weight)

Breastfeed or chestfeed in public

_____

_____

_____

_____

_____

Step 2: Now imagine you were actually going to do these things. How hard would each one be? Keeping this in mind, rewrite each item on a rung of the ladder. Place the easier items on the bottom rungs and work your way up to the harder ones.

Most Difficult

Easy

Step 3: Challenge yourself to do these things in real life. Start with the easier items on the bottom rungs and work your way up as you gain confidence.

SET HELPFUL RULES WITH FRIENDS

Some women worry about what would happen if people knew what they "really" looked like. Enlisting your friends can be a great way to help counter this. Try following these steps for a week or more.

Step 1: If you use any video chat apps with your friends, challenge yourself to be on video no matter what you look like—no make-up, just out of the shower, post-sleepless night, whatever.

Step 2: Challenge your friends to do the same and set a rule that none of you will make negative comments about your own appearance.

Doing this can help you and your friends increase your body acceptance. Remember that one element of body image is your mental image of yourself. By regularly seeing yourself in a more natural state, you start to get used to this image. It becomes less shocking, which helps you accept your appearance more. Additionally, taking pictures and using video apps gives you the chance to really see how lighting, camera angle, and other outside factors impact your appearance. This helps you understand that your appearance is constantly changing, so what you look like in any given moment becomes less important.

UNDERSTAND THE PAST AND MOVE FORWARD

Step 1: Chances are the way you feel about your body today has been influenced by messages you received at a young age. Maybe your mom frequently commented on her own body, or yours. Maybe you had close friends who struggled with their body image. Write about the messages you received about your body when you were a child.

_____

_____

_____

_____

_____

Step 2: Take a moment to reflect on what you wrote. Are you happy with these messages? Do you hope to pass them on to your child? Think of three key messages you'd like to give your child about their body and write them here.

1. _____

2. _____

3. _____

Step 3: Identify three actions you can take to model the messages you want your child to learn. This could be anything from exercising with your child so they learn how to move their body in healthy ways to keeping negative body comments to yourself.

Action 1: _____

Action 2: _____

Action 3: _____

Amazing work! Now do your best to follow through whenever possible. Remember, it's human to forget or fall into an unhelpful action. No one day will shape you or your child's body image. Keep working and you will both learn to feel more comfortable in your skin.

FINDING THE RIGHT LANGUAGE

Sometimes when we are practicing self-love and body appreciation, the words we choose can fall flat. For example, let's say you look in the mirror and think, "I look horrible." You might then try to channel your inner best friend and say to yourself, "You are beautiful." Maybe this will ring true for you, but maybe not. Rather than pushing yourself to think the "right" thing, allow yourself to be honest and find what feels right to you. Practice in the following spaces, noticing the common negative thoughts you have about your appearance and thinking of phrases you can use to talk back to yourself.

Ex: I look so worn out today.

Ex: Of course I look tired; I was up all night. I don't have to look my best every minute of the day. My family still loves me.

_____

_____

_____

_____

_____

_____

_____

_____

Once you have your comebacks, practice using them in your daily life and notice which ones work best. If you need to, keep practicing to find phrases that work for you.

CONCLUSION

I hope that through your work in this chapter you are feeling more at peace with your body, better able to embrace all you love about it, and less focused on the parts you want to change. Remember, you can always revisit these exercises whenever you need a boost. Like self-love more generally, cultivating a positive and healthy relationship with your body takes time.

The next chapter will focus on releasing self-doubt. This will build on what you have already learned about releasing negative judgments about your body and help increase your love and acceptance of yourself.

Bad moments don't make bad moms.

—LYSA TERKEURST

five.
WELCOME SELF-ESTEEM, RELEASE SELF-DOUBT

Let me be honest, self-esteem is not my favorite concept. Too often we tie self-esteem to being better than others, which can lead to comparisons and focusing on our flaws. However, self-esteem does play an important role in building self-love. Remember that being able to recognize and celebrate your accomplishments is part of self-love, and self-esteem can help with this. When you quiet your inner critic and notice your own strengths (rather than comparing yourself to others), you build a strong sense of accomplishment and self-esteem. This allows you to treat yourself with compassion and kindness. The exercises in this chapter are designed to help you do just that.

SELF-DOUBT INVENTORY

Just about every person on the planet has a part of themselves that offers unhelpful judgments and critical messages. Becoming a mom for the first time can shift this part into overdrive. You have an important new role to play, and there is no one-size-fits-all instruction manual. Not only that, but there are often many people around (and online) who offer you "advice" and may criticize or judge you regardless of how amazing you are. Learning a new role combined with contradictory and negative social messages is a recipe for self-doubt.

Look through some of the common worries and doubts and circle the thoughts that seem familiar to you. As you do, remind yourself that these thoughts are signs of doubt and insecurity, not evidence that you are doing anything wrong.

I'm not doing enough to get my body back.	Is my child hitting their milestones on time? I'm probably not doing the right activities with them.	Sleep training worked for my friend, but it's not working for me. What am I doing wrong?
I should be grateful so many people want to come over; I can't say no.	I should have done more research; I don't think this toy/bottle/_____ is best for my child.	I'm not doing enough to document my child's life. I should take more photos, journal, or do something to remember it all.
I should be doing more to help my child learn and grow.	I know children need a schedule. I should be doing more to create a routine.	What's wrong with me? Why can't I figure out what my child needs?
I'm not feeding my child enough/in the right ways.	I should have handled that differently.	What if . . .

GET TO KNOW YOUR DOUBTING VOICE

Now that you're more aware of some of the doubts running through your head, it's time to get more acquainted with what author Anuschka Rees calls your "judgy inner voice." This part of yourself is fueled not by facts but by the understandable worries that come with being a first-time mom and the many contradictory messages about what moms should and shouldn't do.

I recommend you start by giving this inner voice (or "inner critic") a name. If you find your inner critic is overly focused on worries and "what-ifs," you can name it your "anxiety brain," but really "Tiffany" or anything else will do.

Then the next time it shows up, you can say to yourself, "Oh, there's Tiffany again. I don't have to pay attention to what she says."

HELLO
my name is

MAKE FRIENDS WITH YOUR INNER CRITIC

Sometimes, the very act of simply noticing that a thought is coming from your inner critic and being able to name it (i.e., "That is Tiffany talking") can help reduce the sting of those thoughts. Other times, though, you'll need to be able to respond with kindness. On the following lines, see if you can create some compassionate responses. You can even use the thoughts from the "Finding the Right Language" exercise in chapter 4 (page 70) to get you started.

Inner critic thought:

Ex: I can't remember anything anymore!

Compassionate response:

Ex: I've had a lot on my mind today, so it's understandable that I forgot we are out of bread.

_____   _____

_____   _____

_____   _____

_____   _____

_____   _____

_____   _____

_____   _____

_____   _____

_____   _____

_____   _____

UNHELPFUL PATTERNS OF THINKING

As you work to banish doubt and move forward on your self-love journey, it can be helpful to notice what unhelpful patterns of thinking show up for you. Like naming your inner critic, knowing these patterns can help you more easily recognize critical thoughts. Following are some examples of common unhelpful patterns—take a look and see which ones seem familiar to you.

Black-and-white thinking	This happens when we think in extremes and see things as all one way or the other ("I'm a bad mother").
Ignoring the positive	This happens when we focus on supposed "mistakes" and ignore everything else, including all the things we've done right.
Mind reading	This happens when our self-doubts lead us to believe that others are judging us or thinking negatively of us, even though they haven't said anything to indicate this.
Catastrophizing	This happens when our inner critic tells us about all the horrible things that will happen. For example, "My child will forget about me when I go back to work because I will see them less."
Emotional reasoning	This happens when you begin to believe that your emotions are always based on fact. For example, you feel guilty not being able to answer a friend's call, so you believe you did something wrong.

CULTIVATE YOUR INNER CHEERLEADER

It takes more than quieting your inner critic to truly build self-esteem and confidence. You also need an inner voice that helps you notice and focus on the positive.

Step 1: In the space provided, write what you like about yourself. If you get stuck, consider these questions: What positive qualities would my friends/family say I have? What have I done that I am proud of? What am I grateful for? What are my hidden talents?

_____

_____

_____

_____

_____

Step 2: Set aside 15 minutes a day for the next five days (mark it on your calendar). During this time, review your list and make a note of all the times you demonstrated those positive qualities.

DAY 1	DAY 2	DAY 3	DAY 4	DAY 5

Step 3: At the end of the five days, reflect on this process. Was it difficult? Did it make you uncomfortable to recognize your own accomplishments? Are you surprised by what you noticed? Consider how you might cultivate awareness of your successes in the future. Write your thoughts in the space provided.

_____

_____

_____

_____

_____

My inner critic is wrong,
and I am more powerful than it believes.

CREATE YOUR OWN AFFIRMATION

Affirmations can be powerful, especially when they ring true for you. Try to reflect on all you have learned so far and create your own affirmations in the space provided.

EMBRACE FAILURE

Failure. It's such a loaded word. When failure is seen as something to be avoided, it becomes a source of doubt and fear. When failure is embraced as inevitable, it can be a useful teacher. As a first-time mom, you are in for lots of failures. As your child grows, you will have to adapt to your changing life, and it is simply not possible to get things right all the time. To help you embrace failure, take a few moments to consider some past experiences with it (such as not getting a job you applied for) and think about what happened afterward and what you learned from it. Use the space to write a thank-you letter to failure.

Dear Failure,

Thank you for_____

_____

_____

_____

_____

_____

_____

_____

_____

_____

FINDING POSITIVE MOTIVATION

You know that internal voice we have been talking about? When it says you "should be doing more," you often believe it. Sometimes, that voice can even be right.

The trouble is, this judgy voice tends to focus on the negative, on all the ways we aren't "enough." While it can seem like focusing on the negative is the only way to create change, in my experience, people who motivate themselves with criticism tend to be less adaptable in the long term. To figure out if this is true for you, take a moment to write some of the critical thoughts your brain tells you. Then write the impact the thoughts have.

Thought	Impact on me
Ex: I didn't do enough today.	I feel sad and overwhelmed. I want to just go to bed.

Now reflect on what you have written. If your thoughts leave you feeling less motivated or overwhelmed, then it's worth noticing that these critical thoughts aren't doing much for you. The next time one of these thoughts comes up, use the affirmation you created for yourself earlier in this chapter ("Create Your Own Affirmation," page 80) to help yourself remember that you already are enough.

OUTWEIGH THE NEGATIVE

Our brains tend to focus more on negative thoughts and messages, so as you learn to let go of doubt and embrace yourself fully, you will need to practice cultivating positive thoughts and messages about yourself. Think of one to two doubts or worries that are currently bringing you down, and write them in the following spaces. On the other side of the scale, see if you can outweigh those with thoughts that focus on your incredible worth as a first-time mom and overall human.

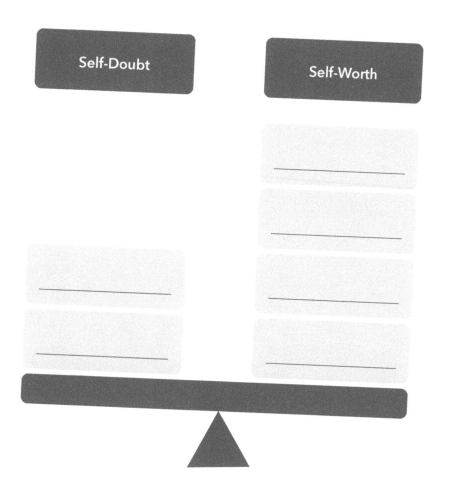

TAKE NOTICE AND RE-CREATE THE POSITIVE

Think back to moments this week when you really felt content. Notice what you were doing, what was going on around you, and who you were with. Now jot down some notes so you can remember.

Situation one: _____

_____

_____

_____

Situation two: _____

_____

_____

_____

Now that you've thought about some elements that help you feel good about yourself, try to re-create the moments when possible.

EMBRACING YOUR CHOICES

Too often in our society, the choices moms make are held up for debate and criticism. Advice on how to be a good parent is often conflicting, and this can leave mothers confused, leading to self-doubt and guilt. One way to combat this is to practice recognizing the reasons your choices make sense. This will help you feel more confident and accept that your choices aren't flaws—they are the result of you doing the best you can in your situation, for your family.

To practice, complete the following sentences. There is no right way to do this; the goal is to acknowledge your choice and recognize why it makes sense and is right for you. If a prompt doesn't fit, skip it!

I have decided to feed my baby _____. This choice

works for me and my family because _____.

In this house, we sleep _____.

This works for me and my family because _____.

I am planning to return to work outside the home (when) _____.

This works for me and my family because _____.

For childcare, we are going to _____. This works for my

family because _____.

MATCH GAME

Following are some common self-critical thoughts you may recognize. Try to pair the critical thought with the more helpful reframe.

Self-critical thought	Helpful reframe
Did I read/talk to/do enough for my child today?	It's not possible to prevent every bump and fall.
I'm so mean for doing sleep training.	There is no right way to feel. I love my child, and that's what matters.
My child fell and hit their head. It's my fault; I should have been watching them more closely.	I am a great mom, no matter how I feel.
I shouldn't be so critical of my spouse.	Sleep training is a choice I made to help my child; I am not being mean.
I should feel more excited about this milestone.	If people are judging me based on my child's behavior in this moment, that is on them, not me.
I feel like I'm not maternal enough.	There is no such thing as "enough." I did my best today with my child.
People must think I am a terrible mother the way my child is screaming right now.	It's okay to feel irritated, and I can find ways to talk to my spouse more productively.

THE TROUBLE WITH PERFECTION

Wanting to avoid mistakes is understandable; however, it is simply not possible to be the "perfect" mother, wife, or friend. Many people strive for perfection because they want to give their best to the people in their lives. Unfortunately, seeking perfection often causes fear, worry, and negative self-judgment.

The more you want to be perfect, the more you notice when you are not. Burning dinner isn't an excuse to order pizza; it means you are failing at everything. Yelling in front of your child isn't just a lapse in judgment; it's a sign that you are a terrible, traumatizing mother. The drive to be perfect can strengthen your inner critic, leaving you exhausted, overwhelmed, and more likely to fall short of your own high standards. This is why it is so important to counter this drive for perfection with gentleness and compassion. Learning to celebrate your successes and treat yourself kindly, even in the face of imperfection, can help keep the negative impacts of perfectionism at bay.

CHECKLIST: YOU MIGHT BE A PERFECTIONIST

The following statements are common characteristics of people who struggle to be perfect. Put a check mark by the ones that fit for you.

- You have very high standards, and even when you achieve 95 percent of your goal, you see it as a failure.

- You easily focus on your own mistakes and those of others. It can be difficult to let something go as "just a mistake."

- You are more motivated by the fear of not reaching a goal than you are by accomplishing something important to you.

- You set unattainable goals for yourself and don't notice when you complete steps toward the goal.

- Even when you know others mean well or are trying to be helpful, any negative feedback feels very painful.

- You avoid starting new things if you aren't sure you will be successful.

Reflect on the statements you checked. Everyone does some of these occasionally, but it is worth noting if you checked more than one or two of these, or if you notice that these patterns impact your daily life. Perfectionism can rob you of so much joy and peace of mind. Moving away from perfection and embracing your imperfect life is an important step toward deeper self-love.

To help you accept flaws and failures, consider revisiting some of the exercises, prompts, and practices in this book, such as "Embracing Your Choices" (page 85), "Allowing Emotion" (page 43), and "Create Your Acceptance Mantra" (page 47). These skills can help you counter your perfectionistic thinking and progress on your journey toward self-love.

SOCIAL MEDIA CLEANUP

For many new moms, social media is both a lifeline that connects to others and a constant source of comparison with people who seem to have it all together. This can lead to self-judgment and feelings of shame. If you have a hunch your social media habit may be fueling your inner critic, I challenge you to try this three-step social media cleanup.

Step 1: On a given day, pay attention to how you feel about yourself when you use social media, and make some notes.

_____

_____

_____

Types of posts that made me feel happy

_____

_____

_____

_____

_____

Types of posts that had a negative impact

_____

_____

_____

_____

_____

Step 2: Mute or unfollow accounts that generate content on the second list—even if this means hiding a friend's account. Curate a social media feed that helps you.

Step 3: Seek out accounts that post the type of content on your first list. These could be posts that contain useful information or are written by other new moms who are honest about their lives. It could even be puppy pictures. The only goal is to make your online space contribute to your well-being.

THE DIALECTICS OF MOTHERHOOD

Motherhood can be full of contradictions. These can feel uncomfortable or confusing and contribute to self-doubt. For example, if you believe you are a strong person, recognizing you need help can be painful. However, you can learn to embrace the notion that opposing ideas or thoughts can be true at the same time. This is called dialectical thinking—the ability to see things from more than one perspective. Rather than seeing the need for help as evidence that you are weak, when you think dialectically (flexibly!), you can see yourself as strong and in need of help at the same time.

Following are a number of dialectics that can show up for first-time moms. Circle the ones that fit for you or write in your own. When these show up in your life, do your best to see both sides.

I can feel angry/tired/
frustrated with my child
AND still love my child.

I can sometimes think that
I am not cut out to be a mom
AND still be a great mom.

I can need help
AND still be capable of
caring for my child.

I can put my family first
AND still be a good friend
to other people in my life.

My child can experience
disappointment AND
feel loved and happy.

I can feel weak AND
still be strong.

BUILD MASTERY OVER MOTHERHOOD

When you become a mom, you may sometimes feel like you have no idea what you're doing. This is okay! Kids have a way of doing the unexpected. While this is normal, it is also really important that you find ways to feel accomplished and capable in your day-to-day life.

In the space provided, identify a goal you would like to achieve and then break it down into smaller steps. This could be getting your kids to eat a vegetable or learning a new skill. As you take each step, make time to notice what you have done and enjoy your accomplishment.

Goal:

_____

Step 3:

_____

Step 2:

_____

Step 1:

_____

QUIET DOUBT WITH BREATH

Your breath is a powerful tool for coping with self-doubt. Focusing on your breath can help you feel more grounded, slow negative thought spirals, and help you reconnect with yourself. Following are three breathing exercises for the times you notice self-doubt. I encourage you to practice these when you're calm so that you're more likely to remember them when you are feeling distressed. Practice each one for 30 seconds at first; you can increase the length of the exercise over time.

1. Hold your hands out in front of you and imagine you are holding a small ball. As you breathe in, expand your hands as though the ball is growing, then bring them back together as you exhale. Repeat.

2. As you inhale, bring to mind a doubt or worry that is troubling you. Hold the thought in your mind. Then, as you exhale, imagine you are breathing out the thought.

3. Pick one pair of thoughts from (or make up your own). Try repeating these phrases as you inhale and exhale.

    a) Inhale: "I am good enough." Exhale: "I don't need to be perfect."

    b) Inhale: "I'm a good mother." Exhale: "My worries don't define me."

    c) Inhale: _____

       Exhale:_____

CONCLUSION

Any path toward self-love means understanding your self-doubts and learning to shift your relationship with these thoughts. This chapter has challenged you to make friends with your inner critic and to learn to counter unhelpful messages. This is challenging, and sometimes difficult, work. I hope you can celebrate the progress you have made so far and show yourself some gratitude for your willingness to be vulnerable and open-minded. The work you have done will help you as you continue to the next chapter, where you will be asked to turn your attention to your own needs.

Taking care of myself
doesn't mean "me first."
It means "me, too."

—L. R. KNOST

six.
PRIORITIZE YOUR NEEDS

Much of the advice aimed at first-time moms relates to their role as a parent and to taking care of the kids. Well, this chapter isn't about any of that. It's all about you! In this chapter, you'll be asked to think about what you want, what you need, and what goals you have for yourself as a person (not as a mother). The goal is to help you stay connected to your whole self and to help you learn to love and care for the parts of you—the work you do, the interests that motivate you, the hobbies you pursue—that can get ignored in the hustle and bustle of parenthood.

NOT JUST A MOM

Becoming a first-time mom can feel all-consuming. It can feel like you need to focus all your energy on your new job, but it is important to remain connected to the parts of yourself that existed before motherhood. In chapter 3, you completed exercises to help you clarify important parts of yourself and think about your values and goals, both as a mom and in your other roles. Now I want you to really focus on the things that help you feel happy and fulfilled. Use the following spaces to write your thoughts.

What makes mom-you feel happy or fulfilled

Ex: seeing my child smile, seeing my child learn something new

_____

_____

_____

_____

_____

What makes non-mom-you feel happy or fulfilled

Ex: having time alone to learn a new skill, spending time with friends, going on a long walk

_____

_____

_____

_____

_____

Now take a moment to reflect on what you have written. There may be similarities or differences—either outcome is great. Throughout this chapter, I want you to keep the second list in mind. This chapter is all about helping you prioritize your needs outside of your family.

GET CURIOUS ABOUT YOURSELF

Take some time to answer the questions and get reacquainted with yourself.

What makes me laugh? _____

What are my guilty pleasures? _____

What am I afraid of? _____

What kinds of things do I like to watch or listen to? _____

What do I like most about my life? _____

What motivates me? _____

What do I do when I am feeling silly? _____

What is my favorite way to move my body? _____

FIND YOUR PASSION

Figuring out what you are passionate about can be tricky. It is also worthwhile to pay attention to what really excites you so that you know what to focus on as you learn to prioritize yourself.

Let's do a little free-association brainstorming. Take a few minutes to think about what kinds of things excite you, motivate you, or fill you with energy. You can pay attention to what's happening in the present or think back to a time when you were excited to learn or do something. Fill the following space with words or images that spark these passionate feelings in you. You can even cut and paste words or images from elsewhere. Feel free to play around with this or add to it over time.

REMEMBER WHAT YOU LOVED

Take some time and think about your life before you became a mother. How did you fill your time? In the following space, write any activities that you enjoyed before your child came into the picture.

Ex: Visit friends without kids

Read a fiction book

Watch a movie

_____ _____ _____

_____ _____ _____

_____ _____ _____

_____ _____ _____

_____ _____ _____

_____ _____ _____

_____ _____ _____

Next, circle the activities you think you would still enjoy but haven't done in the past month. What would you need to do differently in order to enjoy those activities again? Would you need help from your partner, the support of your friends? Challenge yourself to reclaim one activity over the next month. This allows you to plan ahead and look forward to reconnecting with something you once enjoyed.

TIME DIARY

For the next week, I invite you to keep track of how much time you spend taking care of yourself and engaging in activities that help you feel happy and fulfilled outside of your family. Include things like time with friends, working out, studying or working toward a career goal, or anything else. In the following space, write the number of hours (your best estimate) you spend on these activities.

	MORNING	AFTERNOON	EVENING
SUN			
MON			
TUES			
WED			
THU			
FRI			
SAT			

Now reflect on your week. Were there days when you didn't spend any time taking care of yourself? Did you generally only have short periods (30 minutes or less) to dedicate to yourself? Did your "me time" get squeezed in at the beginning or end of the day? If you answered yes to any of these questions, you may want to consider asking for more support and setting some boundaries for yourself.

WHAT DO YOU WANT?

Here is a brief visualization exercise I encourage people to do on a regular basis. It can feel silly and uncomfortable at first because our brains are so programmed to self-edit and identify barriers to getting what we want. This exercise asks you to ignore those barriers and simply reflect on what you want. Even if this feels cheesy, stick with it a bit.

1. Find a quiet space to sit and come to a comfortable resting position.

2. Close your eyes and ask yourself, "What do I want?"

3. Notice what things come up. Don't judge or push away any thoughts.

4. Repeat the question: "What do I want?"

5. Keep paying attention to what thoughts and emotions arise.

6. Now ask yourself, "What do I really, truly want?"

7. Notice what comes up. Keep trying not to judge or push away any thoughts or emotions.

8. Repeat steps 6 and 7 as many times as you would like, but at least twice.

Once you are done, make some notes about what came up. Even if something feels unrealistic, it might have something valuable to offer. For example, noticing the thought "I want to be a famous gymnast" may remind you that you miss the feeling of accomplishment you experienced when you did gymnastics as a child. Noticing that can help you brainstorm new ways of feeling accomplished.

Pro tip: If you have a partner, you can do this exercise together and talk about what comes up for both of you.

CREATE A ROAD MAP TO REACH YOUR GOALS

Focusing on your goals and following your passion requires both the mental and emotional knowledge that you deserve to do so. It also requires a plan. This prompt and the exercise that follows will help you map out a plan to achieve your goals.

To begin, pick a goal you want to work toward. This could be large (building your own business so you can work from home) or something smaller (signing up for a dance class). Once you have a goal, write it down in the space provided. Ex: take a dance class

Now that you have your destination, imagine yourself working toward that goal. What would you need to do? It's okay if you don't know every step you need to take. Take some time to think about it and use the space to jot down what you can. Ex: pick a class, figure out the schedule, arrange childcare

Awesome! Setting a goal and considering some of the steps you need to take can be difficult. You have already overcome one big hurdle by letting yourself think about it rather than avoiding it or buying into the belief that you can't. Now it's time to consider what other barriers you might face. In the space provided, write some things that you think could get in the way of your goal.

Ex: feeling guilty about taking time away, finding time, anxious I won't do well

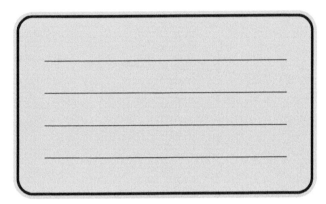

OVERCOMING BARRIERS

Now that you've identified your goal, the steps you'll need to take to get there, and the barriers that could get in the way, it's time to figure out how to overcome the barriers. Think about each barrier you wrote down and begin to consider ways you might get around it.

Barrier	Solution
Ex: I feel guilty.	Remind myself that taking care of me is important.
Ex: I don't have time.	If I lower my expectations of myself (kids don't need a bath every night, I don't need to do everything), I can get back some time.

Amazing work! Now you have built yourself a road map for success. The final step is to picture yourself arriving at your destination. How do you feel about yourself and all you have overcome? What is it like to have reached this goal? Use the space provided to share some of your reflections. You can return to what you have written here to stay motivated as you begin your journey.

_____

_____

_____

COUNTER THE MYTHS HOLDING YOU BACK

Following are several common myths that keep first-time moms from prioritizing themselves. See if you can counter each myth with a more helpful perspective.

I'm selfish if I prioritize my own needs.

Ex: Prioritizing my needs is important to my physical and mental health.
It is required, not selfish.

_____

Others will judge me if I take time for myself.

_____

I can't relax until I know everyone else is taken care of.

_____

I shouldn't need help.

_____

Saying no or setting limits is selfish.

_____

I should focus on how lucky I am as a mother and be willing to sacrifice my own needs.

_____

Something is wrong with me if I need time away or alone.

_____

THE UPSIDE OF BEING SELFISH

"Taking time for myself is selfish."

If I had a nickel for every time I heard this from my clients, friends, or family, I would have . . . too many nickels! So many messages in our society teach people that being selfish is one of the worst things you can be. Women and moms often feel they have to put themselves last in order to be seen as "good." This is a recipe for disaster because the very acts people feel are selfish—asking for help, taking care of oneself, saying no, setting a boundary—are actually important elements of a healthy life and healthy relationships.

When you take time for yourself, tend to your needs, and respect your boundaries, you have more to give to others. Often, doing what feels selfish—working out, reading a book, enjoying a quiet shower—replenishes and protects us so we can give to others willingly. When you don't take care of your own needs, you may still put your effort into caring for others, but you are more likely to feel exhausted or resentful because you are burned out.

My needs and feelings are valid, and
taking care of myself is essential.

YOU NEED PLEASANT MOMENTS

Putting off pleasurable activities until they have been "earned" is a common pattern, especially for people who struggle with self-love. When you have a long to-do list, it can be easy to feel that you don't have time to do something enjoyable; however, we all need to find pleasant moments in each day. Doing this helps us buffer the stress of daily life. Over the next 24 hours, I challenge you to find time (you won't need more than five minutes) to complete as many pleasant events as you can from the list. Use the remaining lines to add more pleasant things you can do in five minutes.

- Take an extra five minutes in the shower to enjoy the warm water.

- Savor your morning coffee or tea.

- Blast your favorite song in the car and sing along.

- Stand outside your front door and feel the warmth of the sun on your face.

- Watch your child sleep.

- Spend five minutes playing or cuddling with your pet.

- Hit snooze once, stay in bed, and enjoy the feeling of warmth and comfort before you begin your day.

- _____

- _____

- _____

- _____

- _____

- _____

- _____

- _____

- _____

SIGNS OF CAREGIVER BURNOUT

Burnout refers to feelings of physical, mental, and emotional exhaustion caused by prolonged stress. Often, we think of burnout in the context of work, but it is possible for caregivers to max out on their capacity to provide support, be it physical, mental, or emotional. Look over the red flags and circle any you are experiencing right now.

Withdrawing from others

Trouble sleeping (not caused by your child)

Physical symptoms like headaches or stomachaches

Changes in appetite

Exhaustion

Increased irritability

Increased anxiety and worry

Feeling sad and/ or hopeless

Urges to be alone

Waking up and dreading the day

Feeling like you need a break

Feeling unmotivated or uninterested in your life

Feeling resentful of your child, partner, or others

If you circled any of the red flags, pay attention. It is human to need a break to care for yourself. Take a moment now to consider how you might ask for help and who around you might be able to give it. Write the names of those people in the following space, and then follow through and ask for help. See "How to Ask for What You Want" on page 112 for tips on how to do this if you are feeling unsure.

_____

_____

If you didn't circle any, that's great. Keep an eye out for these red flags, and if they show up, remember that you need to take care of yourself.

YOUR BODY'S NEEDS

Like many first-time moms, you may play many roles in your life—mom, partner, friend, caregiver, etc. No matter how many parts you play, you are a human being first. This means that you have needs, and learning to attend to those needs is an important part of acting with self-love. Read the statements and check the boxes to indicate whether you are attending to these needs in your life right now.

	Yes	No
I regularly eat at least three times each day.	▢	▢
I move my body regularly.	▢	▢
I tend to my physical health and make doctor appointments as needed.	▢	▢
I get regular sleep.	▢	▢
I stay hydrated.	▢	▢

Take a look at where you checked "no." These are areas that may require more attention. Rather than feeling overwhelmed and trying to change all of this at once, be kind. Being a first-time mom means you have real barriers that get in the way of these needs (children tend to have very little respect for their parents' need for sleep!). Pick one that you feel most motivated to work on and focus this week on ways you can better care for your body in that domain.

GIVE BACK

Many first-time moms find themselves busy taking care of those around them. They may frequently prepare meals to suit their partner's taste, worry about how to include grandparents in key events, work to support their friends, and strive to minimize their partner's stress. While these are loving things to do, if they come at the expense of taking care of yourself, it's time to reconsider and give back some of this work.

Step 1: Make a list of all the ways you are now caring for other adults. Are you picking up dry cleaning that isn't yours, doing the bulk of planning for vacations, arranging video calls with grandparents, or making doctor appointments for other adults? Write it all down.

_____

_____

_____

_____

Step 2: Pick one item on the list and inform the other adult that you will need them to take over or begin helping with this task. Do this gently and consider sharing that you need the time back to focus on taking care of yourself and your child (see "How to Ask for What You Want," page 112).

Step 3: Stick to your word. This can be difficult, so remember that you have a child to care for and that is enough.

MESSAGE FROM A FRIEND

Imagine you have a close friend who tells you she is going to start working toward an important goal. She feels a bit worried it will take time away from her family, yet she also believes it will be good for her. In the space provided, write what you would tell her.

The next time you feel unsure about pursuing your goals, look back at this and remember you deserve as much care and support as others in your life.

HOW TO ASK FOR WHAT YOU WANT

To ask for what you want, you must believe you deserve to get your needs met. It also means risking a "no" from the person you are asking. Hopefully, the work you have done so far in this book has helped you recognize that you deserve to listen to and honor your needs. The following exercise will help you work toward a positive response when you ask people for what you need or want. Review the example and then write your own script.

1. Describe the situation clearly, without blame or critical words, and share how you are feeling.

2. Ask for what you need clearly.

3. Tell the other person how it will also benefit them if they agree.

    For example:

    Sofia, I have been the primary parent staying home with Lorraine on the weekends while you take time for yourself. I am happy you are getting time to care for yourself and feel angry that I do not have any long breaks for myself. Can we set a schedule so that we each have time alone on the weekends? I believe this will help me take better care of myself and feel less stressed, and it will also help me feel valued by you.

    Your turn! Think of a situation where you need to ask for something and write out a script using the three steps listed previously.

    _____

    _____

    _____

    _____

    _____

TO THE MOMS OF RAINBOW BABIES

You may have some different needs if your journey to having a healthy child included pregnancy or infant loss. You may notice that you feel like you are betraying your other child by loving the one in front of you so fiercely. You may also notice increased anxiety and worries about your or your child's health.

If you feel you have not fully processed your past experiences, finding a therapist who is trained in helping parents process these losses can be helpful.

Please also know there are no rules for how you should feel about your loss. It doesn't matter how early you may have miscarried; you are allowed to grieve for the child you lost. It's also fine if you don't relate to any of this. Many people who experience a miscarriage or pregnancy loss are able to view the experience as part of their journey to parenthood and may move through their feelings more quickly. Your feelings are not a reflection of how good a mother you are or how much you wanted the pregnancy.

CONCLUSION

I hope your work in this chapter has helped you feel more connected to your whole self. Though focusing on yourself can trigger feelings of guilt, it is so important that you allow yourself time to do just that. It is only by tending to your own needs that you will be able to care for others in the long run. Next up on the self-love journey: taking time to cultivate and connect to your community. I hope as you move forward and think about your community, you will remember to consider your needs and goals as both a mother and a whole person.

We don't have to do
all of it alone. We were
never meant to.

—BRENÉ BROWN

seven.

CULTIVATE YOUR COMMUNITY

Motherhood can be lonely. Even when you have a wonderful support system, there will be moments—like when you're awake in the middle of the night or caring for a sick child—when you will feel alone. This is normal, and it's important to know that you are not alone in your loneliness. That said, building a healthy support network, one made up of different friend groups, family, neighbors, and colleagues, is one of the best ways to show yourself love. Having a community allows you to feel connection, get support when you need it, and stay in touch with all the different parts of yourself. Maintaining such a community also requires setting healthy boundaries and believing that you are worthy and deserving of the community and relationships you want. A healthy community will help you love yourself—and the more you love yourself, the more you'll be able to build healthy connections. This chapter will help you reflect on your current support network, get ideas for building a stronger community, and discover ways to recognize and set your own boundaries.

TAKE INVENTORY

Take a moment to consider who is a part of your current support network: friends, family, colleagues, neighbors, etc. Then, in the space provided, write the names of the people closest to you in the inner circle and work your way out, with names in the outermost circle representing those who provide less support and/or whom you feel less close to.

REFLECT

What did it feel like to complete the "Take Inventory" exercise (page 116)? For many, simply reflecting on who is in your circle can be helpful, as it can increase your awareness of your network and help you feel less alone. For others, it can be difficult and may highlight the need to build new relationships. Either way, I encourage you to do some more reflection using the prompts.

The people in my inner circle are there because _____.

_____

_____

The types of support I most need from my inner circle are _____.

_____

_____

The types of support I most need from people in my outer circles are _____.

_____

_____

I feel _____ when I look at my support network.

_____

_____

I would like to change my support network in these ways: _____.

_____

_____

MISSING MOM

Becoming a mom for the first time can shift many relationships, realigning things and creating new opportunities for connection. It may be a time when you seek the advice, wisdom, and comfort of your own mother. However, if your mother has died, is sick or impaired, lives far away, or is not a healthy person for you, becoming a mom can reopen old wounds. It is so important that you pay attention to these feelings and allow yourself to sit with and express your emotions. Use the following space to begin this process. You could write a letter to your mother, jot down stories you want to share with your child, or even express feelings of anger and hurt. Listen to yourself and use the space as you need it.

BUILDING YOUR NETWORK: CONNECT WITH OTHER MOMS

No matter how supportive your current network, as a first-time mom it can be helpful to seek out other moms for support. This is especially true if you are among the first of your close friends to have a child. While your friends may be wonderful, it can be helpful to be able to reach out to other moms for understanding and support, and to learn from them.

While you won't necessarily want to become lifelong friends with every mom you meet, if you push yourself to make new connections, you may find a few people who can enrich your life and help you feel less alone on your parenting journey. Following are some tips to get you started. Why not choose at least one or two of these ideas and give them a try? Finding the right people for you can take some time, but building your community is worth it!

* Ask your healthcare provider. Midwives, doctors, and hospitals often have a list of resources they can share. Some hospitals even run new-mom groups. These can be a good starting point for meeting other first-time moms.

* Talk to other parents at the playground, day care, or even at work.

* Check local libraries, community centers, and churches. These places often have a community board with flyers and information, or they may host groups you can join.

* Take a baby yoga, baby swim, or baby music class.

* Search social media. There are many online parenting groups that can help you meet other moms in your area.

a note of caution: Social media can be a great way to connect. I've seen it work for many clients and friends, especially following a move to a new location. However, if you find any group or person on your social media is creating distress or leading you to feel shame or doubt, unfollow them. Also, social media can easily distract you from being present in your in-person relationships, so be careful not to get lost in the scrolling.

NOTICE WHO IS AROUND YOU

In the space provided, write some places where you regularly see other people (the grocery store, neighbors on your daily walk, etc.). In the coming week, challenge yourself to say hello or chat briefly with these people. Even if you don't make a new best friend, you'll get a bit more adult interaction. You may be surprised at how small moments of connection with others can positively impact your mood.

_____

_____

_____

RECONNECT WITH YOURSELF AND CONNECT WITH OTHERS CHALLENGE

One of the best ways to make new friendships is to find people with interests similar to yours. In the space provided, circle the examples that apply to you and brainstorm some more ways you can meet others who share your interests. Then challenge yourself to use one of these ideas to meet new people and connect with your interests.

Church   MeetUp.com group

Local theater/choir/   Community service   Volunteer
music group   organization   work

_____   _____

_____   _____

_____   _____

_____   _____

NEW EXPERIENCE CHECKLIST

Whether you are trying to build a new friendship or deepen an existing relationship, experiencing something new together is a great way to bond. Following are several ideas and space for you to brainstorm as well. Pick one or two and try to do something new with someone in your support network.

Take an art class

Visit a museum
(kid-friendly or not)

Bond over
a podcast

Watch each other's
favorite show

Read a book
together

Try a new restaurant/
coffee shop

Play a board game

_____   _____

_____   _____

_____   _____

_____   _____

_____   _____

_____   _____

LEARNING TO TRUST

For some first-time moms, childcare is one of the biggest obstacles to reclaiming some of their time. While finding childcare can be a task on its own, trusting others (even your partner or close family) can also be difficult, especially if your child had a NICU stay or any health concerns. Allowing yourself to trust others will help you get some of that time back.

Follow the steps, starting small and working your way up to longer periods. Remember, part of self-love is honoring your own emotions, so if you start small you are less likely to be overwhelmed. You are also honoring your need to get out of the house while building trust in yourself and others.

Step 1: List one to two people you can trust to watch your child.

_____

_____

Step 2: Come up with some activities you can do for the time intervals listed and let someone watch your child while you give them a try. Start with shorter periods and then work your way up as you gain confidence.

15 minutes: _____

30 minutes: _____

1 hour: _____

2 hours: _____

_____

SHARE YOUR SHAME

Does this pattern look familiar?

Something bad happens.
(e.g., I wasn't looking and my child fell down.)

Feel guilt/shame.

Decide not to tell anyone about it.
(I don't want them to know what a horrible mom I am.)

Feel lonely and isolated.

So often when something goes wrong, whether we are responsible or not, feelings of shame and worries about judgment lead to isolation and prevent connection. This is especially true when you struggle with self-love and tend to judge yourself harshly.

The good news is that there is a trick to overcoming this pattern: Learn to share your worries, fears, and mistakes with those around you. Doing this gives you the chance to receive support and connection and to see that others aren't judging you nearly as much as you are judging yourself. Sharing with others also shows you that many of them have had similar experiences. This helps you both accept and forgive yourselves and strengthens the bond of friendship and trust by which you are now connected.

Test this out for yourself. Record what you share and how you feel afterward.

Three things I feel guilty or ashamed of that I could share with others	How I feel after sharing
1.	
2.	
3.	

THE VALUE OF SHARING

I often I hear people say that they can't reach out to family and friends because they "don't want to be a burden." There are so many messages in our society that teach people that being a "burden" to others is one of the worst things you can be. This belief can leave you hiding painful feelings and experiences and trying to cope on your own. My guess is that you wouldn't want your friends, partner, or child to feel this way, but you may still feel convinced that YOU are not allowed to be a burden.

Think about the last time a friend confided in you or asked you for support. What did you feel? While you may have felt sad or worried for your friend, you were probably happy they told you. If you were able to offer help and support, you also may have felt some increased self-esteem. You may even have noticed that your friendship grew closer. Here's the thing: Asking for help is often the opposite of being a burden. Sharing your feelings and worries, even painful ones, is frequently a gift to those around us—a chance for them to feel helpful and trusted by us.

DIVIDING THE WORK

Note: This activity is designed for people who are partnered. If you are single, you may still benefit from identifying how certain daily tasks impact you. This information may help you prioritize where to ask for help or, when possible, what areas might be most effective to outsource if you are financially able.

Step 1: Write out a list of daily/weekly tasks that must be done around your home. This list should include necessary tasks (like the dishes) as well as planning and task management (remembering birthdays, buying gifts, scheduling appointments, etc.).

Then in the space next to each item, make a note about how you feel after completing these tasks. As you do this, consider if a task tends to make you anxious, whether you enjoy it, if you can do it easily, and other observations. Have your partner do the same.

My notes	My partner's notes
Laundry:	Laundry:
Cooking:	Cooking:
Shopping:	Shopping:
Writing the grocery list:	Writing the grocery list:

My notes	My partner's notes
Bedtime routine:	Bedtime routine:
Taking out the garbage:	Taking out the garbage:
Planning childcare:	Planning childcare:
Scheduling appointments:	Scheduling appointments:

Step 2: Sit down with your partner and discuss what you both noticed. Let this be the beginning of a conversation that helps you both consider how best to divide up the work. Ultimately, you may both end up taking on tasks you don't enjoy; however, the process of noticing how you feel about each task may help you find ways to better support each other.

ADDRESSING CONFLICT

New parenthood often brings a lack of sleep and increased stress, which is an unhelpful combination when you are navigating major life changes and new responsibilities. Drs. John and Julie Gottman are relationship experts who have studied relationship satisfaction, conflict, and the transition to parenthood in hundreds of couples. They often talk about the need to address conflict, especially regarding the "start-up," or how you begin an argument.

In a "harsh" start-up, a concern is brought up with criticism or blame. For example: "You don't care about me. If you did, you would spend less time on Facebook and recognize what needs to be done around here."

A "softened" start-up, in contrast, focuses on expressing feelings, describing the problem without blame, and expressing a need. For example: "I'm feeling upset and overwhelmed right now" (emotion). "The kitchen needs to be cleaned, and the baby needs a bath" (problem). "Would you help out by taking over bath time" (need)?

See the difference? A softer start-up generally makes it more likely that the other person will hear you without becoming defensive. While big emotions and lack of sleep can make us more likely to use harsh words, practicing a softened start-up is important, in both romantic relationships and friendships.

Next time you notice feelings of anger or worry and want to bring something up with your partner or friends, consider your start-up and make a plan to stay soft.

RECOGNIZE UNHELPFUL BELIEFS

Over the course of their lives, many people develop unspoken rules and beliefs about how relationships should function. Following are a handful of common relationship myths. Circle the ones that show up in your life and list some examples of how they impact you. Knowing the impact of these beliefs can help you reflect on their usefulness to your life. If the myth's impact is negative, you can list an alternative belief.

I shouldn't have to ask. My partner/friend should know what I want/need.

Impact: This belief keeps me from asking for support, and I am often angry when my partner doesn't know what I need them to do.

Alternative belief: I'm more likely to get what I want if I ask my partner directly.

_____

_____

It was my choice to be a single mom. I should be able to do this all on my own.

Impact: I feel ashamed when I struggle to keep up and don't want to ask for help.

Alternative belief: No one can do everything by themselves. I am allowed to need support, and I'm still a great mom.

_____

_____

I am selfish if I say no when others ask something of me.

Impact: I keep agreeing to do things and feel overwhelmed and resentful.

Alternative belief: I'm allowed to say no when I need or want to.

_____

_____

I shouldn't have to negotiate or compromise with others. They should realize that I need help and be willing to step up.

_____

_____

I don't deserve to have my wants and needs met unless everyone else in my family is well and the house is taken care of.

_____

_____

It is selfish to expect others to help me or meet my needs.

_____

_____

My single friends think I'm boring now that I have a child.

_____

_____

ASSERT YOUR BOUNDARIES

Boundaries within a relationship are critically important. They define what you are comfortable with and how you want to be treated. For example, some people really like hugs and others don't. If you aren't comfortable with physical touch, letting your friends know this will help ensure that they can respect your limits. This will help make sure you don't end up feeling resentful or uncomfortable.

Remember in chapter 6 we talked about how to ask for what you want? Well, you can use a similar script when asserting your boundaries.

1. Describe the situation clearly, without blame or critical words, and share how you are feeling.

2. Clearly describe your boundary.

3. Tell the other person how it will also benefit them if they agree.

> For example:
> Mom, last time you took care of Caroline you let her stay up past her bedtime and watch two extra hours of TV. I felt hurt that you didn't follow the rules I set, and I feel anxious about letting her stay with you again. Tonight, I need you to follow the schedule I set so I know you respect my parenting decisions. This will help me know I can trust you and make me feel more comfortable letting her stay with you more often.

Your turn! Think of a situation where you need to set a boundary and write out a script, using the three steps listed previously.

_____

_____

_____

A final note: It is your job to communicate your boundaries to others, and it is their job to listen to you. If you find yourself feeling resentful, noticing that your decisions are ignored, or feeling shame when you aren't sure why, it could mean your boundaries are being violated. If people don't respect the limits you set, that is on them. If the pattern continues, you are allowed to pull back and spend less (or no) time with people who don't respect your boundaries.

IT'S OKAY TO FEEL TOUCHED OUT

For new moms, there is a real struggle to feel like your body is your own. Your child depends on your body for comfort and soothing, and if you carried your child and are breastfeeding or chestfeeding, your child relies on your body for survival. Add to this your partner's desire to feel close to you physically, and it's no wonder so many moms feel touched out. All the demands placed on your body can have you looking at it in a whole new way. Some of this may be positive—you may feel in awe of all your body has done for your child. On the other hand, it's also reasonable if you don't feel like your normal, sexy self. It's important to let yourself feel these emotions and pay attention to your limits. Part of building healthy relationships is setting boundaries and paying attention to your own needs. Remember to sit with and embrace your feelings, as you learned in chapter 1!

YOUR BODY, YOUR RULES

Feeling like you have no control over your body can increase feelings of body dissatisfaction and cause you to pull away from people in your life. It's important for you to communicate to others when you need to be left alone or need a break from physical touch. Listening to your feelings and respecting them and knowing you are worthy of care and having your needs met are all ways you practice self-love.

This can be tricky, and when it comes to your child, you may really have no control—if you are exclusively breastfeeding or chestfeeding, there is not much you can do when your child is hungry. That said, you can set boundaries and limits around physical touch with your partner and others. Fill in the blanks and use this script to help you set boundaries and talk more with your partner to give your body what it needs.

Right now I feel like my body needs a break from _____,

but I do still want us to feel close to one another.

Maybe we/you can do _____ instead?

It is not wrong and I am not mean
when I love myself enough to say no.

SETTING BOUNDARIES WITH YOUR CHILD

If you have a young child, you are likely no stranger to saying no or setting limits on things like how many cookies they get or when they can go outside. However, setting boundaries related to your time and attention can feel totally different. Yes, you are allowed to set boundaries with your child. Doing so is a great way to model healthy boundary-setting for them and helps you move forward on your self-love journey.

Following are some examples of requests your child might make and ways to set limits. Take a look at the examples and write some of your own.

Your child's request/action	Limit-setting response
Ex: Your child asks to listen to a song from *Frozen* again.	You say: I'm so glad you have something you enjoy so much! We can listen to one more song from *Frozen*, your choice. Then we are going to play quietly.
Ex: Your child follows you to the bathroom.	You say: I'm so happy that you want to spend time with me. Right now, I am going to go to the bathroom alone. When I am done, we can play with your LEGO bricks together.

SAY NO

Learning to say no, whether to people or opportunities, can be both very difficult and incredibly important. As a first-time mom, you are spending much of your time and energy taking care of your child and learning as you go. This can be a wonderful time, and it also requires a realignment of your energy and priorities. Learning to say no and set limits will help you with this. Following are a few examples and some blank thought bubbles. Read through the examples and then write in your own, thinking ahead about how saying no will help you feel more prepared next time you need to set a limit.

Friend: "Want to meet up for lunch today?"

You: "I'd love to get lunch with you another time, but not today. I need to get home."

Mother-in-law: "I'll be in the area and am going to pop by to visit the baby."

You: "Actually, today won't work for us, but we'd love you to come by another time when we can plan in advance."

CONCLUSION

You're doing amazing work! I hope the exercises and activities in this chapter have helped you cultivate a healthier and more supportive community for yourself. Motherhood is an incredible journey, and having people to support you and share your joys can help make the 24/7 job of being a first-time mom more manageable. I also hope you have learned how important your continued efforts to practice and increase your self-love are—for you, your family, and your community. There is just one chapter left in this workbook, and it will help you take stock of where you are now and continue to move forward.

In the end, I'm the only one who can give my children a happy mother who loves life.

—JANENE WOLSEY BAADSGAARD

eight.

YOU ARE EXACTLY WHERE YOU ARE MEANT TO BE

You have made it all the way to the final chapter! I hope at this point on your journey, you have made progress toward accepting and being gentle yourself, knowing your value, and recognizing your achievements. I hope you have begun to see the value of self-love in your day-to-day life. This chapter will help you take the work you have done and carry it forward into the future. It will also help you make a plan to continue growing in your self-love and offer some strategies to help you adjust your plan as life changes.

BEGIN WITH REFLECTION

As we begin this final chapter, I encourage you to reflect on your goals. What were they when you began reading this book? How have they changed? Fill in the chart.

What were your goals?	Did you meet your goal? (Yes / Partially / No)	What helped? What got in the way?

What do you notice regarding the goals you met? What about the goals that weren't met? Did any patterns emerge?

_____

_____

_____

How do you feel about what you have accomplished so far?

_____

_____

_____

CULTIVATE GRATITUDE FOR YOU

Take some time to reflect on the effort involved for you to keep up your self-love journey so far. In the space provided, acknowledge your hard work and write some new things you are grateful to yourself for.

NOTICE THE UNEXPECTED POSITIVES

I hope that by taking some time to reflect, you can see that you have made progress toward your goals. Whether you've reached all your goals or are still working on them, I hope that you've also noticed some benefits. On the following lines, write some of the unexpected benefits you've found on your journey toward greater self-love. A benefit could be something you've learned, a skill you've found helpful, or anything at all.

_____

_____

_____

_____

_____

_____

DO THE HARD THING

We've discussed the importance of being gentle with yourself several times throughout this book. Allowing yourself compassion, time to learn, and space to make mistakes is critical. And sometimes, the most important acts of self-love happen when we challenge ourselves to do the hard things we don't want to do, like switching to formula, asking for more help, or exercising when we're tired. All of these things may feel incredibly difficult, even painful, to do. That doesn't mean they aren't important steps to take. Now think about the self-love steps you haven't taken yet. Write them down in the space provided, along with what makes them so challenging.

_____

_____

_____

SETTING A HARD GOAL

Now I want you to imagine that you have been able to do one of the difficult things you named in the previous prompt ("Do the Hard Thing," page 141). How do you feel about yourself after taking this step? How will your life change? Write your reflections in the following space.

Next, see if you can break down the goal into three smaller steps and write them in the spaces. Commit to taking one step this week. If you need motivation to overcome feelings of fear or other barriers, refer to your previous reflection on what it will be like to have taken this important step. Remember, sometimes we need to do the hard things today to make life easier for ourselves tomorrow.

Step 1: _____

Step 2: _____

Step 3: _____

CHALLENGE THE MYTHS THAT CHALLENGE PROGRESS

There are many myths that can get in the way of maintaining a self-love practice. Circle any myths you recognize and try to come up with a response to challenge each one. I've provided examples for the first few, but you should also try to find challenges that feel genuine to you. For the last example, try to come up with your own.

Myth: I've improved my self-love, so now everything should be better.

Challenge: Taking care of myself does not make painful emotions go away; I am just better able to respond to them now.

_____

Myth: I should be able to love myself completely. If I am struggling to love some part of myself, I have failed.

Challenge: I am still learning to fully embrace myself, and that is okay.

_____

Myth: I've figured out how to set boundaries with my partner, so I should be able to set boundaries with everyone else now.

Challenge: _____

_____

Myth: I spent time figuring out how to be kind to myself, but it is selfish to take more time away from my child to continue working toward my personal goals.

Challenge: _____

_____

Myth: _____

Challenge: _____

_____

_____

ONE CHANGE AT A TIME

Very often, we can get caught up in the idea that growth and self-improvement should be linear. It would be great if this were true, but that is just not the case. Life will provide many opportunities for your self-critical voice to show up and for feelings of guilt or other worries to get in your way.

To combat this, it's important to pay attention to the small changes that show you how far you've traveled. In the space provided, reflect on the progress you've made so far. Are you noticing your inner critic more, asking for help more often, or saying more positive things to yourself? Whatever changes you have made, write them and keep adding to the list as you go. You can turn back to this when you need a reminder of how far you have come.

_____

_____

_____

_____

_____

REMEMBER TO EMBRACE IMPERFECTION

As you move forward, it will be important to continue to work to quiet that inner critic and embrace your status as an imperfect human. In the diagram that follows, fill in the blank spaces with different endings to the sentence "I am still a good parent if _____." You can also repeat this with various prompts to help you remember that your value as a parent/friend/artist/other role is not based on one thing.

I am still a good parent if . . .

. . . my child had a tantrum at the grocery store.

. . . I didn't accomplish anything on my to-do list.

. . . I lost my temper.

LOVING-KINDNESS MEDITATION

Find a quiet and comfortable place to sit and begin by taking several breaths. Gradually bring your attention to your breath, noticing each inhale and exhale. Once your mind is focused, picture your child in your mind. Now, speaking to your child, say each phrase out loud or in your mind, sending these wishes to your child.

> May you feel loved.
> May your body remain safe from harm.
> May your mind be well.
> May you be able to learn and grow.
> May you be filled with ease and happiness.

Repeat these as many times as you like. Notice and allow any feelings that arise. Then bring your attention back to your breath. Turn your attention inward and focus on yourself. Say each phrase out loud or in your mind, this time sending these wishes to yourself ("May I feel loved," "May my body remain safe from harm," etc.).

Repeat this as many times as you like. Notice and allow any feelings that arise. When you are ready, return your attention to your breath. Notice your inhale and exhale. Begin to notice any physical sensations, like the feel of the chair beneath you or the touch of the air on your skin. Expand your attention to the sounds around you. Open your eyes and notice where you are. Take a moment to simply be present.

EMBRACE THE MESS

When developing a self-love practice, people often think they need to change who they are or fix how they are feeling. While many of the exercises in this workbook can help you create change, remember that back in chapter 3 we discussed the importance of accepting where you are. Acceptance is crucial because what we don't accept tends to stick around. When we do the work of self-love with the goal of getting rid of an emotion or fixing ourselves, it can backfire. Rather than focusing on the goal of change, it is important to embrace the reality of your life, even in stressful moments, and to treat yourself with kindness and compassion. Try the following practice when you find yourself struggling in your daily life.

* Bring to mind a situation that is causing emotional pain, or notice what is happening in the moment that is painful.

* Become curious. Where is there discomfort in your body? Notice whatever physical sensations are present.

* Become curious about your emotions. What feelings are present for you? Allow yourself to connect to these emotions; don't push them away.

* Close your eyes. Bring your right hand over your heart and your left hand across your stomach as though you were holding a child. Take several deep breaths this way, offering yourself kindness and gentleness with your embrace.

* Speak to yourself (out loud or in your mind) with a gentle and supportive tone, acknowledging what you are feeling. Say, "This is a difficult situation, and you are doing the best you can. These feelings are not permanent."

* Allow yourself to remain present. You do not need to move to fix your feelings. If you feel you have made a mistake, acknowledge that with compassion. Say, "I am imperfect and deserving of kindness simply because I am."

LITTLE EYES AND EARS ARE WATCHING

While I hope you approach the path of self-love with the goal of learning to love yourself for yourself, doing this will also help your child immensely. This is because your little one is watching you. They are learning so much from your words and actions, and not just the ones you direct toward them. For example, when you make negative comments about your body, saying, "I hate my stomach, I have such a pouch," they learn that it is normal to be critical of their own body, and they begin to learn what is and is not acceptable.

This process repeats in so many ways—with your emotions, your actions, and all the little ways you show yourself love (or don't). So on the days you feel selfish, like you are being a "bad mom" for taking care of yourself, use this for some extra motivation. Your self-love journey is for you, but it is also for those around you.

Please know that this is not meant to shame you for any of the times you have made negative comments about your body, your emotions, or yourself in front of your child. No one can model perfect self-love at all times. That is not an attainable goal, and perfection is not what your child needs. It is okay for them to see you struggle. It will also be valuable for them to watch you treat yourself with kindness and compassion, accept your emotions, and forgive yourself for mistakes. What will matter in the long run is the pattern they see. Simply by working through this book, you are on your way to giving them a wonderful model of self-love!

In this moment, I can be patient with myself.
I have come so far, and I am still learning and growing into who I want to be.

RED FLAGS

Building self-love over the long run requires regular practice. It also means being aware of signs that you have been ignoring or neglecting some aspect of yourself. It is normal to have phases in life where you focus more on one thing (learning to be gentle with yourself) and end up neglecting something else (taking care of your physical health).

Following is a list of some areas that frequently get neglected and some examples of warning signs. Look these over and add your own warning signs for each so you know what to watch for in your own life.

Not taking care of your physical body
- Feeling tired and not able to focus
- _____
- _____

Not challenging negative comparisons to others
- More frequent worries that you are not doing enough; feeling sad
- _____
- _____

Not asking for support
- Feeling lonely or resentful
- _____
- _____

Not thinking about your values and goals
- Saying yes when you want to say no
- _____
- _____

Ignoring aches and pains in your body
- Avoiding your own doctor appointments
- _____
- _____

COPING WITH PUSHBACK

As you work to embrace self-love, asking for what you need and asserting boundaries, you may get some pushback from those around you. Maybe you are asking your partner to help more with housework. Perhaps you are no longer allowing your in-laws or your parents to stop by without notice. Whatever changes you have made to create space for yourself, it's okay. You are allowed to make changes for your own well-being.

Now for the hard part. Others are also allowed to have feelings about these changes, and they don't have to be happy. It's important to remember what your responsibility is when you set boundaries and what others' responsibilities are. Take a look at the chart and consider the differences.

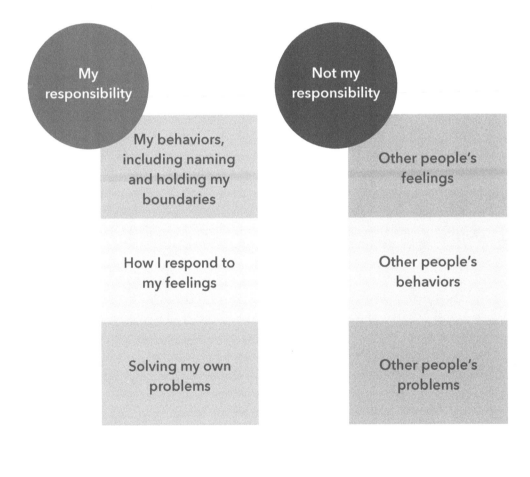

My responsibility

My behaviors, including naming and holding my boundaries

How I respond to my feelings

Solving my own problems

Not my responsibility

Other people's feelings

Other people's behaviors

Other people's problems

Now I want you to consider ways you are currently taking responsibility for other people's reactions to your efforts to move toward self-love.

Ex: I am quick to drop one of my boundaries (not helping with bedtime) if I feel my partner is tired.

_____

_____

_____

Brainstorm some alternative ways to respond that allow you to uphold your boundaries or need for support.

Ex: Say to my partner: You look really tired. If it would be helpful, we can trade. I can do bedtime so you can relax, and you can take over the morning routine for me.

_____

_____

_____

HOW FAR HAVE YOU COME ON YOUR SELF-LOVE JOURNEY?

Following is the self-love quiz from chapter 2. Take a moment to answer the questions again and see how much your score has changed.

1 = Strongly disagree   2 = Disagree   3 = Undecided   4 = Agree
5 = Strongly agree

1. I do not believe I deserve love and support from others.

    1   2   3   4   5

2. I would not talk to others the way I talk to myself.

    1   2   3   4   5

3. I focus more on my failures as a parent than I do on the ways I am succeeding.

    1   2   3   4   5

4. I feel selfish when I try to take care of my own needs.

    1   2   3   4   5

5. I have a hard time telling others no.

    1   2   3   4   5

6. I try to avoid looking in the mirror, and when I do, I focus on my flaws.

    1   2   3   4   5

7. I struggle to ask for help, even from my partner and close friends.

    1   2   3   4   5

8. I am not sure I deserve help.

    1   2   3   4   5

9. I often think that I am a "bad mom" and take any challenges or negative behaviors my child displays as proof of my failures.

   1   2   3   4   5

10. I have a hard time accepting a compliment with a simple "thank you." Instead, I tend to minimize it or point out my flaws.

    1   2   3   4   5

SCORING:

0 to 10: Really nice work! Keep it up and you will build an even stronger sense of love and self-compassion, which will help you throughout your personal and parenting journey.

11 to 30: You have a good foundation, though you struggle at times to accept yourself and can be a harsh critic. This is part of the journey. Try not to judge yourself and continue to work toward deeper self-love. Revisit the pages that spoke to you and reach out to others for support

31 to 50: Today you are focusing much of your attention on your perceived flaws and inadequacies. You may feel this will motivate you to change or do better, but it doesn't work that way. You are an amazing person and deserve to fully embrace yourself, flaws and all. You also deserve to be kind to yourself. Change doesn't happen overnight, or in a straight line. You will have ups and downs. Keep working!

SELF-LOVE CHALLENGE

Now it's time to challenge yourself. Begin by planning one self-love practice a day for the next week. This can be anything—reading an affirmation aloud, taking a walk, asking for help, or completing an exercise from this book that has been helpful. You can do something different each day, or the same thing. Add one intentional act of self-love to your calendar each week. See if you can make it all the way to week 4!

If the plan falls through, that's totally fine. Be flexible with yourself and adjust as needed. There is no failure here.

Week 1: One intentional act of self-love a day

SUN	MON	TUES	WED	THU	FRI	SAT

Week 2: Two intentional acts of self-love a day

SUN	MON	TUES	WED	THU	FRI	SAT

Week 3: Three intentional acts of self-love a day

SUN	MON	TUES	WED	THU	FRI	SAT

Week 4: Four intentional acts of self-love a day

SUN	MON	TUES	WED	THU	FRI	SAT

FINAL REFLECTION

For your final exercise, I invite you to take one last look back. How has your work in this workbook impacted you? Do you feel a greater sense of self-love? If so, how does this affect you physically, emotionally, mentally, and in your relationships? Use the space provided for some final reflection. You can also turn back to this should you struggle with self-love in the future. Being able to remember its impact on you today may help you gain motivation to return to self-love when you need it.

_____

_____

_____

_____

_____

_____

_____

_____

_____

_____

_____

When I dare to be powerful—
to use my strength in service
of my vision—then it becomes
less and less important
whether I am afraid.

—AUDRE LORDE

a final word

Congratulations! I hope the previous pages have been helpful to you, and I hope you will return to the exercises and skills you have learned many times in the future. You deserve so much more than to put your self-love on autopilot.

If the journey to this page has been challenging, I thank you for showing up for yourself. For first-time moms, it takes a lot to focus on your own needs. I have asked you to be willing to sit with painful emotions, embrace difficult thoughts, and take action despite your fears. I know this has not always been easy, but neither is parenting—or life, for that matter.

Moving forward on your journey, you are bound to face new challenges. Your child will continue to grow, challenging you to adapt as their needs change. You will undoubtedly face loss, sadness, failure, and disappointment. You are only human, and that reality of life doesn't spare any of us. When things feel difficult, I hope you will return to what you have learned.

I am also hopeful that your life will be filled with more joy because of the work you have done to prioritize yourself and to learn to embrace yourself fully. So many people struggle to take the steps toward self-love that you have, and yet here you are! You did it! This work will pay dividends for you and your family for years to come. You'll be able to face the many uncertainties of life, model self-love for your children, and continue to build and maintain a healthy community, all from a place of self-acceptance and love.

Finally, I hope you continue to grant yourself the time to read and explore new books and tools to help you move forward. I have learned to care for myself better through so many different media—books, yoga, time with friends, and interesting classes, just to name a few. Keep learning and growing and know that you are worthy.

resources

PERINATAL MENTAL HEALTH

MGH Center for Women's Mental Health
WomensMentalHealth.org
Run by the Massachusetts General Hospital Center for Women's Mental Health, this page offers information on women's mental health across the life span.

Postpartum Progress
PostpartumProgress.com
This site is filled with useful information, downloadable resources, and help locating support.

Postpartum Support International (PSI)
Postpartum.net
In addition to a provider list and general information, PSI offers a helpline and weekly online support groups run by peer support specialists.

Kleiman, Karen. *Good Moms Have Scary Thoughts: A Healing Guide to the Secret Fears of New Mothers.* Sanger, CA: Familius, 2019.
This book, made up largely of illustrations, is a quick and useful read with tips and stories to help you feel less alone.

Kleiman, Karen R., and Valerie Davis Raskin. *This Isn't What I Expected: Overcoming Postpartum Depression.* Boston: Da Capo, 2013.
This book provides tools and in-depth information on postpartum depression and recovery.

TRAUMATIC BIRTH EXPERIENCES

Birth & Trauma Support Center
BirthandTraumaSupportCenter.org
This site offers a resource list of mental health providers along with peer and partner support groups.

Birth Monopoly
BirthMonopoly.com
This is a great resource for those who have experienced obstetric violence or wish to find ways to support changes to maternity care.

Improving Birth
ImprovingBirth.org
This organization offers resources for those healing from a traumatic birth experience.

PREGNANCY/INFANT LOSS

Helping After Neonatal Death (HAND)
HANDOnline.org
HAND has many local chapters, and you can often find support groups tailored to your experience. Many chapters also run a helpline.

Pregnancy After Loss Support (PALS)
PregnancyAfterLossSupport.org
PALS runs online and in-person support groups for moms who are pregnant after a loss. Their website also has valuable information and articles that may be helpful.

PREGNANCY RECOVERY

It is important to consult with your medical provider to discuss any concerns you have about your health and physical recovery following childbirth.

Every Mother
Every-Mother.com
Every Mother exercise programs are designed for pregnancy and the postpartum stage.

The Whole Mother
TheWholeMother.com
This site offers information and support for pregnancy and postpartum health.

University of Utah, Women's Health
Healthcare.Utah.edu/womenshealth
/gynecology/postpartum-pelvic
-floor-disorders.php
The women's health section of the health care home page has great information to help you better understand pelvic floor disorders.

BODY IMAGE

Rees, Anuschka. *Beyond Beautiful: A Practical Guide to Being Happy, Confident, and You in a Looks-Obsessed World.* **New York: Ten Speed Press, 2019.**
This self-help book is packed with great information to help you appreciate your body and worry less about your looks.

Taylor, Sonya Renee. *The Body Is Not an Apology: The Power of Radical Self-Love.* **Oakland, CA: Berrett-Koehler Publishers, 2018.**
TheBodyIsNotanApology.com
This book and its accompanying website offer useful information and a community dedicated to self-love.

PARENTING SUPPORTS

Frank, Hillary. *Weird Parenting Wins: Bathtub Dining, Family Screams, and Other Hacks from the Parenting Trenches.* **New York: TarcherPerigee, 2019.**
This book is a fun and useful resource filled with real-life examples of creative hacks, tested by real parents.

Guber, Tara Lynda, and Leah Kalish. *Yoga Pretzels: 50 Fun Yoga Activities for Kids and Grownups.* **Illustrated by Sophie Fatus. Bath, UK: Barefoot Books, 2005.**
Yoga Pretzels is a set of cards that offers unique, simple ways to engage in mindfulness with your child.

Pollak, Susan M. *Self-Compassion for Parents: Nurture Your Child by Caring for Yourself.* **New York, NY: Guilford Press, 2019.**

This useful book is filled with exercises to increase your self-compassion and helpful anecdotes to help you remember you are not alone in the struggle of parenting.

LGBTQ PARENTS

Gay Parents to Be
GayParentstoBe.com
This site offers information and resources for gay and trans parents, including information on funding IVF and finding support.

Gay Parents Magazine
GayParentMag.com
More than just a magazine, this website includes information on local resources and support groups.

ADVOCACY AND SUPPORT FOR BLACK WOMEN

Black Mamas Matter Alliance
BlackMamasMatter.org
The website for this activist organization offers information and resources to improve Black maternal health.

Black Women Birthing Justice
BlackWomenBirthingJustice.com
The website for this collective offers resources and information to empower Black women and birthing people, including listings of local providers of color.

references

Ayers, Susan. "Delivery as a Traumatic Event: Prevalence, Risk Factors, and Treatment for Postnatal Posttraumatic Stress Disorder." *Clinical Obstetrics and Gynecology* 47, no. 3 (September 2004): 552-67.

Clark, Abigail, Helen Skouteris, Eleanor H. Wertheim, Susan J. Paxton, and Jeannette Milgrom. "My Baby Body: A Qualitative Insight into Women's Body-Related Experiences and Mood during Pregnancy and the Postpartum." *Journal of Reproductive and Infant Psychology* 27 (2009): 330-45.

Gottman, John M., and Julie Schwartz Gottman. *And Baby Makes Three: The Six-Step Plan for Preserving Marital Intimacy and Rekindling Romance after Baby Arrives.* New York: Three Rivers Press, 2007.

Hayes, Steven C., and Spencer Smith. *Get out of Your Mind and into Your Life: The New Acceptance and Commitment Therapy.* Oakland, CA: New Harbinger Publications, 2005.

Linehan, Marsha M. *DBT Skills Training Manual.* 2nd ed. New York: Guilford Press, 2014.

Locke, Edwin A., and Gary P. Latham. "The Development of Goal Setting Theory: A Half Century Retrospective." *Motivation Science* 5 (2019): 93-105.

Mednick, Sara C., and Mark Ehrman. *Take a Nap! Change Your Life: The Scientific Plan to Make You Smarter, Healthier, More Productive.* New York: Workman Publishing Company, 2006.

Stuart, Scott, and Michael D. Robertson. *Interpersonal Psychotherapy: A Clinician's Guide.* London: Hodder Arnold, 2012.

Thompson, Joel Kevin. "Body Image: Extent of Disturbance, Associated Features, Theoretical Models, Assessment Methodologies, Intervention Strategies, and a Proposal for a New DSM Diagnostic Category—Body Image Disorder." *Progress in Behavior Modification* 28 (1992): 3-54.

index

acknowledgments

I don't have enough space here to name all the people who have helped me put this workbook together. First, I have to acknowledge my wonderful husband, who always believes in me more than I believe in myself. His love has given me courage. This would not have been possible without the support of my family, including my parents and a wonderful crew of sisters, cousins, aunts, and uncles, to whom I am eternally grateful. I am forever indebted to my teachers and mentors—thank you for challenging me. To my friends, I love you all and am grateful for the many ways you contributed to this workbook. Finally, to those who have trusted me to care for you, I am forever grateful, and I am better because of our work together.

about the author

ELSA ROJAS, PhD, PMH-C, first became interested in caring for pregnant and postpartum people during her master's program at the University of Houston, where she learned how empowering and important the process of pregnancy and birth can be. She also began to understand the many ways the process of creating a family can leave parents feeling anxious, depressed, and traumatized. For over a decade, this knowledge has fueled Elsa's passion for perinatal mental health and inspired her to become certified in Perinatal Mental Health by Postpartum Support International.

Elsa's research focuses on trauma, including trauma following childbirth. Elsa also gives talks to students, medical trainees, and her community to educate people on the importance of the perinatal period and the need for mental health support—before, during, and after pregnancy or pregnancy loss.

In private practice, Elsa works primarily with new parents, providing supportive and evidence-based care aimed at helping her clients build the life they want and recover from past traumas. She is also clinical assistant professor at Stanford University Medical School, where she works with teams providing LGBTQ+ affirming care, supporting individuals in their recovery from trauma, and providing dialectical behavior therapy.